# Business Planning for Special Schools

## A Practical Guide

Caroline Coles and Richard Field

**David Fulton Publishers**

London

David Fulton Publishers Ltd
Ormond House, 26–27 Boswell Street, London WC1N 3JD

First published in Great Britain by David Fulton Publishers 1997

Note: The right of Caroline Coles and Richard Field to be identified
as the authors of this work has been asserted by them in accordance
with the Copyright, Designs and Patents Act 1988.

*British Library Cataloguing in Publication Data*
A catalogue record for this book is available from the British Library

ISBN 1–85346–471–6

Typeset by FSH Print and Production, London
Printed in Great Britain by Bell and Bain Ltd, Glasgow

# Contents

# Acknowledgements

Thanks to Robert Hancock for reading and editing the manuscript.

Thanks to Helen Field for preparing numerous drafts and rewrites.

We are indebted to David Banes, head teacher at Meldreth Manor School, for allowing us to include his business plan within this book.

We must also thank John Adams, Director of Contract Services at Scope, for his permission to include material related to the wider organisation.

*Preface*

# Business Planning for Special Schools

Special school head teachers and their governing bodies are anxious to ensure that their pupils are provided with the best educational opportunity possible within the funds that are available to them. Improving school effectiveness by creating an environment in which pupils and teachers achieve effective learning is about management development. The term 'Local Management of Schools' (LMS) as opposed to 'Local Financial Management' was coined by the consultants Coopers and Lybrand to emphasise that educational as well as financial improvement should be expected from the process.

The notion of producing a business plan in a special school may be seen by many educationalists as inappropriate. In commerce and industry business plans are viewed as powerful, indeed essential, agents in providing an organisation with a clear purpose, and direction that is clearly understood by all. This clarity of purpose along with a focus on raising efficiency and improving cost effectiveness within a business plan framework, is also a concept adopted by the public sector industries such as the health service. The same can, and should, be achieved in education.

LMS and local management within the special school are enabling the school to become increasingly autonomous. Schools are buying in services and receiving very varied support from LEAs. Heads and their governing bodies can be more 'businesslike' in their approach to introducing change and development in their schools, as many more financial and management decisions can now be taken close to the point of delivery.

Schools need to re-examine their patterns of expenditure, consider how each spending decision they make contributes to the educational goals of their pupils, and consider whether there are other things they could do with their funds which would serve the goals and aims of their service better.

This book has four key elements:

1. It advocates a system of business planning for special schools to support them within the LMS framework, or it can equally support the independent school managing its own budget.

2. It outlines a process that can support schools in their short-term or long-term planning of expenditure and development within a clear framework.

3. It suggests a process of consultation, of production of a business plan, and of implementation and review which is effective within a special school.

4. It includes a case study of how one individual special school managed the process. This is not put forward as a perfect model for others to follow, but as an example of how the process can be organised and managed effectively.

This book is based upon the practical process which was undertaken by the schools, colleges and education services within Scope (formerly the Spastics Society). Scope is a voluntary organisation active across England and Wales, and is the largest charity for people with a physical disability in the UK. The aim of Scope is to create, in partnership with others, an environment in which any person with cerebral palsy or an associated disability may determine his or her own way of life.

Integral to the charity are its education services, and the business planning process initiated by the principal education officer was supported and encouraged by senior managers within Scope, who believed it to be an effective contribution to financial understanding, useful training for managers, and of assistance in the process of gaining a better understanding of how financial decisions can impinge upon the quality of effective provision.

The book also recognises the 'added value' factor of the special school sector in comparison with that of a primary or a secondary school, which also changes the nature of business planning. Aspects of this are related to:

- size;
- variety;
- individual pupil need;
- disability groupings;
- greater expectation and involvement of parents;
- the challenge to offer the broadest relevant curriculum;
- the variety of staff involved;
- the nature of support services indicating the need for part-time staff – therapists, medics, psychologists, etc.;
- the residential nature of some provision.

This level of complexity, linked with the perception that many schools are under threat, presents a challenging period of change for special education. The business planning mechanism has never been more needed to support the special school sector in clarifying its aims, advertising its provision, developing into a more community-based resource, and enabling it to perform to the highest standards.

# Why Use This Book?

This book is a practical guide to business planning within special schools or related services.

The book explores a practical way of addressing business planning in a special school. It draws upon the experiences of the authors in developing a process based upon a case study within Scope's educational service. It provides examples of ways in which the budget and other planning processes can be structured and co-ordinated involving staff and governors using key tools and techniques appropriate for the process.

The book contains:

1. A number of questions which will help the reader develop the process of business planning within their organisation.
2. Key processes and tools used to develop a business plan.
3. An example business plan completed in respect of a special school.
4. A set of overhead transparencies which can be used for briefing others in business planning.

*Chapter 1*

# Introducing Business Planning

This chapter introduces business planning by identifying some of the factors which have lead to its widespread adoption. The potential benefits of introducing business planning and characteristics of a successful plan are also outlined. The chapter concludes with the introduction of a business planning model.

Business planning is not new, at least not in the private sector. For as long as entrepreneurs have needed to secure finance, they have had to persuade would-be shareholders or lenders of the merit of their case, normally via the submission of a business plan.

Whilst business planning has traditionally been undertaken for the 'whole' organisation seeking finance, this is increasingly being extended to smaller units within organisations. These units are often established as 'business' or 'trading' units enjoying considerable freedom over how they operate but with a requirement to achieve a target level of profitability, or to meet certain standards. Used in this context the plan is normally aimed at securing the 'permission' of senior managers within the wider organisation for a proposed course of action.

In the public and voluntary sector, business planning is comparatively new, being one of a number of widespread responses to the changes of the last two decades. This period has seen a significant shift towards a more commercial and 'businesslike' approach to managing public and voluntary services, encouraged by legislation concerning compulsory competitive tendering, the creation of internal markets, market testing, etc. There has also been a general increase in the level of devolved responsibility, with many organisations, including schools, developing new structures and arrangements for managing services. Included within this change process is the adoption of purchaser/provider arrangements, where the provider unit must frequently operate as a business unit. Irrespective of the detailed arrangements for operating these units, which can vary significantly, there is a common need to define their purpose and ensure the services they offer are attractive to the customers and purchasers they seek to serve. Without recognising this change the survival of these units may well be at risk, as was the case when Local Management of Schools was introduced and many local authorities created business units for curriculum advice, personnel, finance and local authority inspection teams. Where once these simply provided 'uncharged-for' services to schools, they now had to sell their services in sufficient quantity to secure income to survive.

Within local education authority (LEA) schools there is now much clearer and greater responsibility and freedom to operate, but in the knowledge that a failure to perform in a 'businesslike' as well as in an educational sense could ultimately cause the school to fail.

Whilst voluntary sector schools have always been dependent on contract income from LEAs, social services and health departments, there is an increasing pressure to tailor provision to meet the needs of purchasers and individual pupils. OFSTED reports indicating the levels of 'efficiency' and value for money are becoming increasingly important to the purchaser. A failure to offer appropriate high-quality provision at an acceptable price is likely to lead to a loss of contract income, dwindling school rolls and increased unit costs. Unless an organisation is prepared to fund the resulting income shortfall from non-contract sources, the school may be forced to close.

Business planning provides a means for ensuring that the direction and operation of the school is appropriate to the needs of pupils and other stakeholders. Effective use of the process should lead to resources being deployed in the most appropriate way, value for money should be achieved, and the school should constantly develop.

## *Defining business planning*

There are as many definitions of business planning as there are organisations. Martin and Smith (1993) define business planning as 'the activity of preparing your organisation for events that will influence its future'.

Knight (1993) described the rational model of planning with its cycle of analysis, objective and strategy setting leading to implementation and monitoring. Business planning is one approach falling within this model.

Figure 1.1 gives the definition of business planning used within this book.

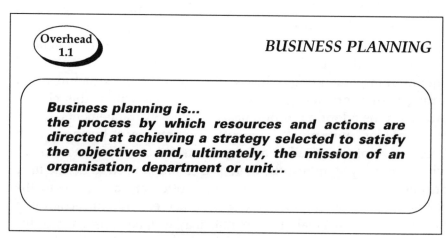

**Figure 1.1** Business planning definition

This definition extends beyond that offered by Martin and Smith (1993), recognising two important dimensions: firstly, the identification of an appropriate direction for the school or service; and, secondly, the deployment of resources in a way which should ensure that this direction is followed.

If business planning works well it will become an integrated part of the management process, and a constant but not dominant part of school life.

The most tangible outcome of the planning process is the business plan, defined by the Local Government Management Board (LGMB, 1991) as 'a statement of the actions and resources required by a business to sustain and grow its activities'.

*Defining the business plan*

Most organisations prepare business plans to persuade decision-makers to invest new money or allocate scarce resources in a particular way. Uppermost in the decision-maker's mind therefore will be concerns about whether the actions proposed in the plan appear logical given the context, and whether the hoped-for results are desirable and realistic.

The definition in Figure 1.2 recognises that the business plan needs to persuade decision-makers of the merit of proposed actions. One important means of doing this is by including a summary of the environmental context within which the school or service is likely to be operating, together with an assessment of its ability to do so effectively.

---

**Overhead 1.2**                              *BUSINESS PLANNING*

*A business plan is...*
*a document which describes a set of clear actions needed to achieve a desired outcome set, within a summary of the environmental and organisational context in order that the reader may be assured of its realism and integrity...*

---

**Figure 1.2** Business planning in special schools

The time period covered by a business plan varies by organisation but normally involves three to five years, with the first year being highly detailed. The process of completion includes consideration of the overall purpose of the school (mission), what it wishes to achieve (objectives), and the means for doing so (strategy).

Some organisations prefer to have a strategic (long-term) plan and a business plan which is then focused on implementation of the strategic plan. The approach to business planning advocated here encompasses both the long- and short-term dimensions within a single process and document.

In approving a course of action the organisation is in effect confirming that the plan is both educationally and commercially sound. What makes commercial sense, at least in the short term, might be ill-advised educationally, and those approving the plan will need to consider the impact such proposals will have on the learning experience of both current and future pupils.

## Benefits arising from business planning

Whilst organisations introduce business planning for a wide variety of reasons, the benefits they are seeking are common. The extent to which they are realised depends on the quality of the plan and the process used to generate it. The potential benefits are identified in Figure 1.3.

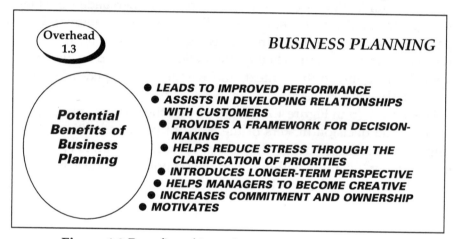

Figure 1.3 Benefits of introducing business planning

## Characteristics of a successful business plan

Ultimately the success of a business plan is likely to be judged in terms of whether the school or service achieves the objectives it sets itself.

For some managers, a success factor can simply be whether the plan is accepted by those evaluating and approving it. Given the possible managerial target to gain this immediate measure of success, it is important that those evaluating do so thoroughly. This evaluation involves separating two strands. Firstly, the appropriateness of the specific objectives and strategies contained within the plan and, secondly, the structure, content, persuasiveness and overall quality of the document.

There is a need to ensure that those involved in business planning have a shared understanding of what constitutes a good business plan. This helps those writing it to pitch the content correctly, and those evaluating it to benefit from having a framework against which to make a judgement. The characteristics included in this framework and the relative weight given to these will vary. Within Scope, for example, education services developed criteria clustered into two main areas: qualities and content. These reflected the shared concerns and priorities identified by their education team. Implicit within these shared concerns was a need for the plan to be written in a way which was clear, well-structured, and sufficiently detailed to allow those evaluating it to make an informed judgement.

To ensure effective business planning a robust process is required, and an important factor in this is the adoption of a clear model as shown in Figure 1.4. Whilst this appears to be a neat set of stages, each being completed before the next starts, the reality is inevitably more complex, frequently requiring those planning to revisit earlier stages of the process. Whilst the first attempt can be of enormous assistance to the organisation it can often take three years of business planning before the document reaches a high and well-refined standard. This is because of the need to collect new data, gain familiarity in the use of tools, and gain confidence in managing the school as a commercial as well as educational entity.

*Establishing a business planning model*

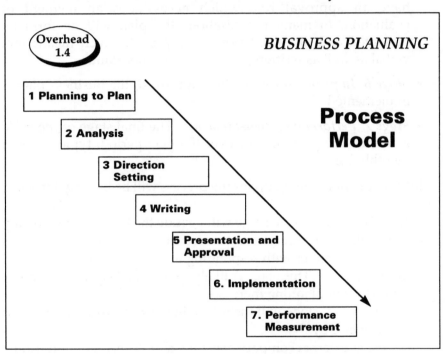

**Figure 1.4** Business planning model

In this model there are seven stages, each of which is outlined below and developed in detail in Chapter 3.

- *Stage 1. Planning to plan* – If the process is going to be effective it is vital that it is planned. This will include setting planning timetables, determining who should be involved, identifying the target reader, etc. In particular, attention in the first year must be paid to assessing and meeting the training needs of all those involved – a process which, if undertaken via a structured staff development programme, will normally take two days.

- *Stage 2. Analysis* – Business planning requires data analysis, both quantitative and qualitative, although in cycle one this is often limited due to poor availability of data. This analysis includes consideration of the strengths and weaknesses of the school or service, external influences on the school, data on pupils and purchasers, alternative providers, etc.

• *Stage 3. Direction setting* – Appropriate actions flow from a clear understanding of the purpose of the school, what it intends to achieve and how. This stage involves defining the school mission, setting objectives and determining strategies.

• *Stage 4. Writing* – The time taken to write a plan is frequently underestimated. This leads to the preparation of the document being rushed, and the consequent failure of a good proposal simply through poor presentation.

• *Stage 5. Presentation and approval* – Business plans may be prepared for a variety of audiences, one of which will normally have an approval role which necessitates an element of evaluation. In many organisations the plan will be formally presented and discussed prior to approval, which means that verbal as well as written presentation is important.

• *Stage 6. Implementation* – Once approved, the business plan is implemented.

• *Stage 7. Performance measurement* – The final stage of the cycle is to measure performance over the plan period, typically on a monthly basis.

In subsequent planning cycles the process will be broadly the same but:

1. The 'Planning to plan' stage will include the identification of any new tools and techniques to be used in the next cycle of business planning, together with responding to the development needs of those involved. This stage is likely to become less demanding as experience in planning increases.

2. The 'Analysis' stage will include a review of historic and current performance by:
   (a) using external comparisons, for example examination results and league tables; and
   (b) internal comparison with the existing business plan.

This stage is likely to become increasingly demanding as more historical and external data becomes available, and those planning develop more confidence in the process and demand still further data.

*Chapter 2*

# Developing an Approach to Business Planning

In Chapter 1 a distinction was made between business planning as a process, and the business plan which is the main tangible output. Poor business plans are often a result of inappropriate planning processes. This chapter raises a number of issues which it is suggested should be considered at the outset, being discussed at a briefing meeting of those responsible for business planning. The purpose of this meeting would be to determine an appropriate, consistent approach to the planning process and secure the commitment of those involved. In addition to considering each aspect of the plan in detail it might also be necessary to:

- define business planning as a process and the business plan as a document;
- introduce participants to the potential benefits of business planning;
- outline the main stages of the planning process.

There is no universal approach to business planning; each school and service needs to develop an appropriate process, relevant to their context. Figure 2.1 provides a framework for this.

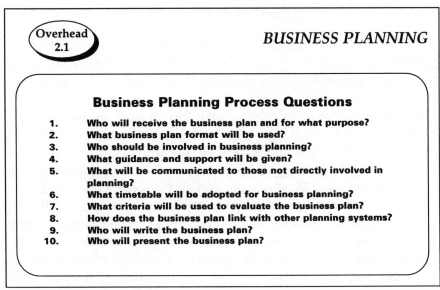

**Figure 2.1** Business planning process questions

This chapter considers each question in more detail, summarising the factors involved, and offers options for consideration.

## Question 1: Who will receive the business plan and for what purpose?

Business plans can make an important contribution to effective school management and be a valuable means of building the support of staff, governors and parents. Each of these stakeholders will have a different purpose for reading the plan, different needs and expectations, and different levels of understanding of education.

Normally the business planning team will tailor the content of the plan to the likely readers of the document, which can prove problematic where there are many different stakeholders. In this case it is worth identifying those considered to be the primary readers.

If the plan is to be circulated widely there may be concerns regarding confidentiality, as there may be information which should not be shared with some readers.

The target readers, in a school context, include:

1. The governing body, who have a role in influencing the direction of the school, approving budgets and evaluating the performance of the school and its managers.
2. Staff who, in addition to understanding the direction of the school, need to be aware of planned targets and standards and their part in achieving them.
3. Local education authorities, purchasers of services or other funding bodies who need to be able to assess proposed fee levels or funding requests.
4. Parents, who increasingly wish to understand and be involved in the school or service. The plan should help them reach a judgement about the performance of the school and be part of the wider process by which their needs and desires are understood and responded to.
5. OFSTED, which is concerned to see whether the school is professionally managed in terms of efficiency and value for money.

The plan should recognise that the wider community is also a potential recipient of the plan as part of the process of involving business partners, recruiting staff or seeking additional resources.

## Question 2: What business plan format will be used?

It is useful to adopt, or design, a plan format early in the process to help shape the thinking and writing of those preparing the document. Although there can be no universal format, some organisations do develop a 'house style' or at least a preferred format which can be used. Most schools and services enjoy the freedom to develop a tailored format, although this can prove difficult until business planning experience has been gained. The elements within a business plan can be clustered into three main sections.

1. *Analysis* – This normally involves a review of performance, including an assessment of organisational strength and weakness, an environment analysis including the market-place and competitors, detail of the services offered and the

opportunities and threats faced by the school or service.

2. *Direction* – This includes details regarding the purpose of the school or service, what it is intended to achieve over the period of the plan, and the means selected for achievement.

3. *Implementation* – This includes the arrangements for implementing the plan, the budget, the approach to monitoring performance and the contingency plan.

Appendix A includes a format which has proved successful in schools and can be used as an initial framework.

## Options

1. Adopt the framework included in Appendix A, recognising this might need amendment to reflect the specific school or service.

2. Select a framework from another source, although this might use different terminology and will also need amendment.

3. Allow a framework to emerge during the planning process, although there is a danger that key elements are missed or sequenced in a way which lessens the plan's persuasive quality.

4. If available adopt a format already used within the LEA or wider organisation, which in some contexts might be mandatory. Where an existing format is optional this should be considered, as adoption of it will assist the decision-makers and ensure that the key data required by them is included within the plan.

Business plans are more effective where they are widely owned and understood. This factor alone might well justify the involvement of all staff, governors, parents and other stakeholders. In the context of the special school this involvement is potentially wide including, for example, speech therapists, occupational therapists and physiotherapists. Whilst this breadth of involvement provides a range of perspectives and experience which should enrich the planning, a larger group will make the process more difficult to manage and the plan will take longer to complete. A further factor may be confidentiality, which can arise where, for example, consideration is being given to altering the staff structure and those potentially affected are involved in the planning process.

Whilst there may be some staff who resent being involved in this management process, teachers are now seen as elements in whole-school management, and it can be argued that they should have involvement in planning.

Many governors and parents are seeking more effective mechanisms to become meaningfully involved in a school or service, and business planning can be an ideal means of facilitating this.

Options include:

1. Using the management team for the planning process with formal staff, governor and parent consultation.

2. Creating a small project group comprising staff and governor representatives.

*Question 3:*
*Who should be involved in business planning?*

Whilst it is possible for the head teacher to plan without the significant involvement of others, the resultant document will probably be weak and not be owned by governors, staff or parents. This possibility is not offered as an option, nor in most instances is the other extreme, this being to involve all staff, governors and parents. This is time-consuming, difficult to manage and not a practical option.

*Question 4:*
*What guidance*
*and support will*
*be given?*

Successful business planning requires a considerable investment of time and effort, particularly in the initial cycle as people coming to this often take time to learn the new skills and become confident in their application. There is a need to gain confidence in utilising a new vocabulary, planning tools, process and document format. More importantly, business planning requires a different method of observation and analysis, which can be challenging for some of those involved in the process.

Strategies for guiding and supporting staff during the planning process need to be appropriate to the number of staff involved, their experience and competence.

**Options**

The options for supporting the process include:
1. Commissioning a staff development programme for all those involved in business planning.
2. Using a facilitator to keep the process moving, act as a 'sounding board' and provide technical support.
3. Supplementing in-house skills in specific areas, for example finance.

*Question 5:*
*What will be*
*communicated to*
*those not directly*
*involved in*
*planning?*

The introduction of business planning can create quite a stir within the school or service. For those who are not involved there may be fears, fuelled by rumours, which can lead to tension between those 'inside' and 'outside' the planning process. The extent of this tension is significantly reduced by early communication regarding the planning process.

In addition to deciding what needs to be communicated prior to planning, a further decision needs to be made regarding the extent to which ongoing proceedings are to be reported outside of the planning group. If thoughts and discussions are to be shared widely during planning, attention needs to be given to how this will be managed. If sharing is not to take place it is important that those involved treat proceedings as confidential.

**Options**

Two decisions need to be made, the first regarding initial communication. Options include:

1. Briefing all staff and governors about the planning process and the time-scales involved, together with explaining the extent to which those not directly engaged in planning will be able to contribute to or discuss the outcome. It should be recognised that staff have the potential to contribute both in respect of their particular expertise (as a speech therapist, for example), and more generally regarding the whole service.

2. Extending the briefing to include giving some reassurances about the reasons for introducing business planning and the benefits which it is hoped will be gained. Business planning can lead to radical proposals for school or service management, and this should be explained to all staff. Care needs to be taken not to give reassurances which limit the options considered at a later stage.

The second decision regards communication during the planning process, the main options being to:

1. Issue progress reports with the intention of regularly briefing those not directly engaged in the process.

2. Circulate briefing papers at predetermined points in the process, inviting comments in respect of key elements of the business plan. This has the dual benefit of communicating progress and testing out some of the thinking which will underpin the document. It is also likely to increase the commitment to the final direction of the school or service.

3. Keep proceedings confidential until the final plan is issued. In many organisations this would prove difficult and inappropriate, being contrary to the prevailing style of management and likely to fuel the concerns of the staff involved.

Business planning tends to fill the time allocated to it. It is advisable at the outset to limit this by preparing a timetable and setting a deadline for plan submission . This timetable will vary depending on the context and approach selected, an example of which used by the education service within Scope is included in Chapter 6.

One factor in determining the timetable is the number of people engaged in the process, either directly or indirectly. The more people involved the longer it will take, particularly if stakeholder views are sought.

A second factor is whether there is an existing deadline for completing the document, for example a scheduled meeting of the governors, or budget and school development plan submission dates.

As senior staff, in particular, are likely to be involved in the planning process, the extent and timing of other demands on their time will be a factor.

A final consideration will be the pattern of planning activity, which can range from a single concentrated event to an extended process over a number of months. This in part will be influenced by the preference of the planning group for treating this as a separate activity or as an agenda item at regular meetings.

*Question 6:*
*What timetable will be adopted for business planning?*

**Options**

Two decisions need to be made. The first decision regards the time frame, with the main options being to:

1. Complete the business plan in a single burst of activity. This has the attraction of encouraging focus and rapid completion, but does not allow time for reflection and can prove impractical.
2. Spread the business planning process over a longer period using a series of meetings or events.

The second decision regards whether business planning should be seen as a discrete activity. The main options are to:

1. Undertake business planning at specially-convened meetings where this is the only item on the agenda.
2. Include business planning as an agenda item for regular management team meetings, in which case care needs to be taken to ensure that immediate day-to-day concerns do not assume a greater importance than the business plan.

*Question 7: What criteria will be used to evaluate the plan?*

The prime reason for developing the business plan is to present to the governing body a clear, cohesive service plan which is properly costed. Following evaluation the governing body will be required to give approval or return the plan for further consideration.

The quality of future planning processes will be improved if the current plan has been subject to rigorous evaluation and feedback.

One key aspect of plan evaluation concerns the financial element and the need to ensure that those evaluating have sufficient competence. Whilst schools will normally have such expertise represented within the governing body, this may not be the case in other organisations where the decision-maker may be a line manager.

One evaluation issue which can arise is the different expectations of planners and decision-makers regarding the purpose, format, content and presentation of plans. It is recommended that at the outset the criteria against which the plan will be evaluated are identified, along with the process for providing feedback. Examples of the criteria and evaluation forms used by Scope's education services are given in Chapter 6.

**Options**

The options for identifying the evaluation criteria and feedback process include:

1. Asking decision-makers to identify the criteria and evaluation process which they wish to adopt.
2. Tasking the planning team to identify the criteria and evaluation process and then agree these with the decision-makers.

Whichever approach is adopted, and the preference normally is for the second option, this should be completed prior to starting the business planning process.

To avoid multiple and possibly contradictory planning systems it is advisable at the outset to identify existing planning systems, their purpose and potential for being linked. Examples of these include the school development plan, budget, information technology plan and staff development plan, each of which might have different planning cycles and processes, involve different planning groups and use different formats and terminology. Unless carefully managed, plans will become repetitive and confusing, with a lack of clarity as to what goes into which plan.

Whilst the case for linking, if not integrating, plans appears strong, there are a number of factors which need to be considered before deciding the approach to be taken.

One consideration is whether there is a logical sequence or progression between different plans, in which case this will need to be recognised in the timetable. One approach might be to prepare the business plan first, as this is where the direction of the school or service is considered, which should be a strong influence on other plans. However, there is a need for the business plan to reflect the resource requirements of other plans and there is a case for these feeding into it. In practice the planning timetables will need to be co-ordinated to allow each plan to influence the other.

In linking or integrating the plans a consideration should be whether the purposes served by any of these will be weakened as a result.

The breadth of plans will probably be different, and this can cause problems in linkage. For example, budgets are traditionally of one year's duration whilst the business plan covers between three and five years. School development plans, in practice, often focus on development more than on the whole school, whereas the business plan is prepared on a whole-school basis.

As the business plan should include the budget, this assumes integration with the budget being approved as part of the business plan. This is consistent with the budget being considered a financial expression of the physical resources needed to pursue the business plan. The practice in many organisations of having separate plans and budgets is not recommended, as it can lead to changes being made to the budget which are not then reflected in altered activity levels within the business plan.

*Question 8: How does the business plan link with other planning systems?*

**Options**

Options include:
1. Co-ordinating the production of the business plan, which includes the budget, with other plans. Separate documents exist, but there are clear links between them.
2. Integration of these plans in a single document, which assumes that these are approved at the same time.

Whatever happens business planning should not be seen as a

separate process: a degree of linkage is required, the extent depending on the context.

*Question 9:*
*Who will write*
*the business plan?*

Writing business plans is more difficult and normally takes longer than expected. The benefits of good analysis and thinking can all too easily be lost if writing is rushed, drafts not discussed or the document poorly proof-read.

Within the overall timetable sufficient time needs to be allowed for writing, recognising that several drafts might be required, with time between to allow for checking, editing, etc. Writing is the last stage in preparing the plan, so any breaking of earlier deadlines will affect this stage, particularly if there is a firm final deadline for submission.

Writing is a skill which is not necessarily present in all managers, so consideration should be given as to who actually writes the document.

A final factor to consider is the extent to which those involved in the planning process can critically appraise the document. It can prove helpful to ask someone else to read and comment critically on early drafts.

**Options**

Options to be considered with regard to writing include:
1. Allowing a time contingency within the overall production of the plan to allow for slippage in the earlier stages.
2. Production of a writing schedule, indicating when drafts are due, who will read them and when comments are required for the next edit.
3. Identifying someone to read the document who is sufficiently knowledgeable to challenge what has been written and the extent to which it meets the criteria identified at the outset of the process.

One approach which is not recommended is to share the writing, as this normally leads to inconsistency, poor flow and unnecessarily long documents.

*Question 10:*
*Who will present*
*the business plan?*

This question is relevant only in those organisations where decision-makers require or give the opportunity for oral as well as written presentations.

In preparing for oral presentation consideration should be given to the forum in which this will be received, which in a school context will probably be a governors' meeting. The intended forum will have expectations regarding who presents, in many cases this being the head teacher, or head of service.

Given that the plan is intended to be persuasive, a factor to be considered should be the communication skills of the presenter. The plan will need to be presented in a simplified and clear manner, allowing decision-makers to be persuaded of the logic of the proposed actions. The content, which will be a summary of the plan with key points stressed, will be greatly enhanced by the use of overhead transparencies and other visual aids. Any temptation simply to read from the plan should be resisted.

A further factor concerns other impressions which will be conveyed through the approach to presentation. If the desire is to show clear, firm leadership then head teacher presentation might be the most appropriate. If, however, there is a need to show wide ownership and team commitment then using other members of the management team might be appropriate.

If, as is often the case, there will be some questions to be answered following the presentation, the approach to this will need to be considered. A reasonable decision-maker expectation is that each planning team member should understand the plan to the extent that they ought to be able to answer any question regarding it, albeit to different levels of detail. In preparing for the presentation, discussion should include establishing how such questions are to be handled.

**Options**

The options for presentation include:
1. Head teacher or head of service to present the plan and answer questions.
2. Head teacher to present the plan but the team to answer questions which arise.
3. Senior members of staff present with the rest of the team providing answers. The head teacher in this option takes a back seat, getting involved only if circumstances require.

*Chapter 3*

# Preparing the Business Plan – Analysis

Business planning differs from other types of planning in the extent to which the external environment features in both the analysis and the way that the direction of the school or service is developed.

The business plan differs from other planning documents in its persuasive nature, and in that it relates to all the activities of the whole school or service rather than being simply about new developments.

Initially appearing straightforward, business planning may be treated superficially. One way of minimising this risk and ensuring that business planning is undertaken in a rigorous way is through the use of appropriate planning processes or tools.

There are many processes which can be used in business planning, ranging in complexity, sophistication and appropriateness to the public and voluntary sector. The number included in this book have been kept to a minimum, being those judged particularly useful in the education sector.

Over time, planners should develop mastery of planning tools and processes, and an understanding of when and how to use them. All the planning tools included can be used in the first cycle of business planning, although these may require some data which is new to the school. In subsequent planning cycles further tools can be added, in turn requiring more data and possibly staff development.

Figure 3.1 identifies six key questions to be considered in the analysis stage of business planning. This chapter contains processes or tools which will assist in answering these questions, and which will provide the information needed to write the 'Analysis' section of the business plan.

*Question 1: What do we know about the performance of the school or service?*

A natural starting point for analysis is to understand the current performance of the school or service. As performance will be monitored during the year, answering this question should be straightforward, although possibly involving more extensive analysis than previously undertaken.

**BUSINESS PLANNING**

**Analysis – Six Key Questions**

1. What do we know about the performance of the school or service?
2. What do we know about how we operate?
3. What do we know about our environment?
4. What do we know about our customers and services?
5. What do we know about competitors or alternative providers?
6. What do we know about opportunities and threats?

**Figure 3.1** Analysis – six key questions

**The process**

The performance of the school can be analysed by completing the following four steps.

- *Step 1 – Identify current key objectives.* Usually there is a small number of objectives key to the development, if not survival, of an organisation, normally found in the current business plan. In the first cycle of business planning it will be necessary to identify key objectives from other sources, e.g. the school development plan or budget.
  *Example:* 'Ensure that the service breaks even financially each year.'
- *Step 2 – Identify other measures of performance.* In addition to the key objectives there may be other important performance measures which should be identified.
  *Examples*: Occupancy levels.
  Average annual unit cost of a pupil.
- *Step 3 – Analyse performance.* Having determined the means by which performance is to be measured, data will need to be gathered. This is used to compare actual performance with existing plans and previous performance. Depending on the measures selected it might be possible to compare performance with similar organisations, as outlined later in this chapter.
  *Examples:* Projected surplus/deficit against budget for the current year.
  Average unit cost per pupil over the last five years.
- *Step 4 – Consider implications.* The final step is to stand back from the analysis and consider the overall performance of the school and how this has changed over time.
  *Example:* If the financial performance is being considered it should be clear whether the financial objective is likely to be achieved in the current business plan or budget, and whether this performance is improving or weakening over time.

**Tips**

1. Select a small number of key objectives and performance measures, and consider them in depth.
2. When comparing financial data over a number of years, remove the effect of inflation from the figures used.

*Question 2: What do we know about how we operate ?*

An important aspect of business planning is self-knowledge, which can be developed using a strengths and weaknesses audit. Identifying strengths and weaknesses leads to an understanding of what the organisation is good and bad at, and where it has an advantage or disadvantage over other organisations (Martin and Smith, 1993). This audit should draw upon the views of the head teacher, governors, management team, staff, pupils and parents. It should also include what others have said about the school, including OFSTED reports, and social service and other inspections and visits. In future years consideration should be given to extending involvement to other stakeholders on a wider basis.

Many organisations incorporate the strength and weakness audit within a broader technique known as SWOT (strengths, weaknesses, opportunities and threats). However, experience indicates that the tool is easier to use and more effective if the strengths and weaknesses audit is separated from the analysis of opportunities and threats, as considered in Question 6.

The strengths and weaknesses audit tends to generate a considerable number of responses, some of which may be insignificant, and some of which are over-emphasised or when challenged may not be true. Attention should be focused on factors which:

1. Are strengths or weaknesses compared with other schools or services. For example, IT equipment may be considered a strength where it is better than that used by another school or service.
2. Benefit, or cause difficulty for, the school or service. For example, playing fields can be a strength if they benefit the school through improved sporting facilities leading to a reputation for competition and/or personal success. Ultimately this might attract pupils and, in the independent and voluntary sector, allow higher fees to be charged and more specialist staff to be employed. However, if no real advantage is gained from having quality playing fields they might actually prove to be a weakness, due to the cost of maintenance.
3. Are significant in their impact. Continuing the example of playing fields, significance might be measured in higher occupancy, increased fees or additional staff resourced. Significance could also manifest itself in local and national promotion of the school, improved learning experience of pupils and the ease with which quality staff are attracted to the school.

**The process**

There are three steps involved in determining the strengths and weaknesses to be included in the business plan.

- *Step 1 – Identifying the factors.* The first step involves identifying factors without considering their importance or impact, and often results in a long list of factors which vary in significance.

   *Example:* – Strengths
   - Ability to tailor service to individual pupil needs.
   - Open for 52 weeks per year.
   - Good reputation.
   - Level of staff expertise.
   - Nicely decorated.
   - Convenient for railway station.

- *Step 2 – Testing the factors.* Test each factor by asking three questions:
   (a) Is the factor a source of strength or weakness when compared to other schools or services?
   (b) Does or could the factor yield a benefit or cause difficulty?
   (c) Is the factor considered significant in terms of its impact?

   *Examples:* A school may be 'nicely' decorated when compared with other schools, but this might not prove to be a major factor in parents choosing this school.
   Convenience to the railway station might be irrelevant if staff, parents or pupils do not travel by train.

Where any question is answered with 'NO' it is unlikely that the factor will feature in this business plan. However, it is worth considering whether any rejected factor should be monitored, as a change in purchaser preferences, competitor behaviour or government policy could make it relevant.

- *Step 3 – Testing perception.* As it is common for there to be different perceptions regarding strengths and weaknesses, it is worth testing each factor to see if other stakeholders, for example pupils or parents, agree that it should be included.

   At the end of this process a short list of important strengths and weaknesses should remain which can then be included as short statements in the business plan.

   *Example:* 'The staffing structure is expensive and doesn't meet the changing needs of children with increasingly complex physical and medical needs.'

**Tips**

1. Ensure that each factor is stated in specific terms. A statement that 'our staff are a strength' is too general and should be questioned. For example, is it all staff, specific staff groups or particular members of staff that are a strength? In what way are they a strength? Why is this important to the school or service?

Explored in this way, 'our staff are a strength' might become 'the administrative staff are a strength due to the welcome they give parents and the way they promote a positive image of the school'. This is rather different from all staff being considered a strength in all respects!

2. Accept that some factors may appear to be both a strength and a weakness. For example, although administrative staff might be a strength in how they welcome visitors, they may be unduly distracted by this, with routine work suffering and errors being made.

3. Recognise that some strengths or weaknesses might prove to be irrelevant when challenged. A general belief that the school is good because of the quality of staff might not be supported by OFSTED.

4. Establish the extent to which each factor is likely to increase or decrease in importance over time.

## *Question 3: What do we know about our environment?*

A characteristic of the business plan is the analysis of the environment within which the organisation operates. Whilst other types of plan may take this into consideration, it tends to be given greater importance in business planning.

Although the environment is complex, ever-changing and difficult to predict, the business planner should aim to share with the reader their current understanding of what the future might hold. Considering the environment should ensure that the direction outlined in the plan is appropriate, and required changes in operation can be identified early. Although it is unrealistic to expect to anticipate all environmental changes, the more obvious ones can often be identified and therefore considered.

Whilst some environmental influences are fairly predictable, for example the impact of legislation due to take effect next year, others are much less so, particularly those relating to political statements or local authority change. Whilst some influences will affect the first year of the plan, others will impact later. There may even be a few which will not impact until after the end of the plan period.

A final consideration is that environmental influences can at the same time but in different ways impact on society, education in general, purchases, users and competitors as well as the school or service. When planning, the potential implications for all these stakeholders need to be considered, as directly or indirectly they impact upon the school or service.

### The process

There are many different ways of undertaking environmental analysis, most of which use a framework which comprises the main sources of environmental influence. A common one used is PEST: political, environmental, social and technological sources (Barnard and Walker, 1994). As legislation tends to be of particular importance to the education sector, it is more appropriate to consider an analysis using a SPELT framework. Each element of this is outlined below.

- *Social influences* focus on trends and changes in society. Examples include population numbers and structure, morbidity, mortality, changes in family life.

  *Example:* Children are being born and surviving with much greater levels and complexity of disability. This has implications for equipment investment, and staff development.

- *Political influences* arise at local, national and European levels. These includes changes in funding mechanisms, priorities for education, and current policy emphasis.

  *Example:* The creation of unitary authorities as a result of local government review has many implications, including the impact on contract management. Although the total number of pupils should remain the same , more purchasing authorities will be involved. As a consequence additional time will be required to build and sustain relationships with purchasers, including visits, inspections, etc.

- *Economic influences* include inflation rates, funding levels and interest rates which impact on expenditure, and income from all sources.

  *Example:* There is increasing pressure on the budgets of all public sector bodies, leading to purchasers questioning the cost of service provision and their share where children are funded on a bi- or tri-partite basis. Schools need to understand the cost of different activities involved in providing a service to a child.

- *Legislative influences* relate to statutes, a few of which might affect the school or service directly, some more generally apply to the education sector, whilst others apply to employers including schools.

  *Example:* Mini-bus regulations, and in particular those regarding seat belts (regulations February 1997), have restricted the opportunity for many children to take part in educational activities. Seating and the use of seat belts for children with severe physical disabilities has meant considerable adaptation to school mini-buses.

- *Technology influences* are felt in many different ways. Some developments directly affect the education process, for example communication and vision aids. Other technological changes have less direct effect, impacting on the administration and general operation of the school.

  *Example:* With the changes in computer technology, children who communicated previously through a member of staff (e.g. pointing to a word or symbol board) can now use advanced technology to operate machines or computers with synthesised or typed speech.

**The process**

It is suggested that a three-step process be used to undertake environmental analysis.

- *Step 1 – Identifying influences.* This step identifies influences which might impact on the school or service in each of the SPELT areas.
- *Step 2 – Impact analysis.* This step involves exploring each influence by asking the following questions:
  1. What might this influence generally mean for the education sector?
  2. What might be the impact on purchasers and users of the school or service?
  3. What might this influence mean for those schools or services which we identify as competitors?
  4. How might this influence impact on our school or service?

  By asking these questions it should be possible to isolate those influences which if left unaddressed would impact significantly on quality, demand for places, fee levels, etc.
- *Step 3 – Assessing influences.* The final step is to group the environmental influences as follows:
  1. Influences which do not appear to impact significantly on the school either now or in the future. These can be omitted from further consideration.
  2. Influences which will significantly shape this business plan and should be reflected in the plan objectives and strategies.
  3. Influences which are unlikely to impact in the early years of the business plan but warrant monitoring.

**Tips**

1. Recognise that many environmental influences can be attributed to more than one source.
2. Identify trends in the environment, for example decreasing funding levels as well as one-off changes such as the implementation of legislation.
3. Consider involving a wide stakeholder group including governors, who being external to the school can bring different perspectives.

*Question 4: What do we know about our customers and services?*

The success of an organisation can be measured by the extent to which the services it offers meet the needs of the customers it seeks to serve. This relationship is shown in Figure 3.2.

Effective business planning should lead to the school or service meeting the needs of customers. The importance of this has grown due to the introduction of local management, purchaser/provider relationships, and the direct linking of financial resources to the number of children on roll. Alongside this, attempts to increase

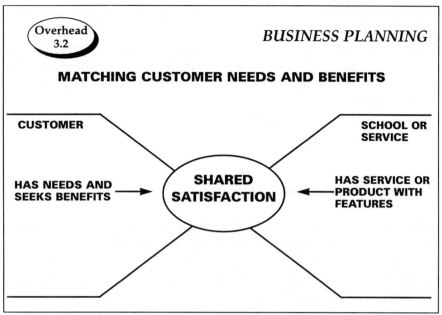

**Figure 3.2** Matching customer needs and services

parental choice make the flow of pupils less predictable and increase the pressure to compete between schools or services.

A failure to meet customer needs may result in them going elsewhere, or services containing features which are not needed, making the school more expensive than others which have a better match of needs and services.

Understanding the match between needs and features is relatively easy when the person using the service also pays for it and will determine whether to use the service again.

Within the public and voluntary sector the relationship between service providers and customers is rarely clear. In the special school context pupils, parents and purchasers are involved in a complex relationship. The school or service must recognise the needs of all these stakeholders. In general terms:

- *Pupils* have educational needs and in many instances health and social needs.
- *Parents* are concerned to see that their child is receiving the services which they believe are needed.
- *Purchasers* seek to ensure their statutory objectives and polices are discharged. Meeting the needs of purchasers is more difficult where there are multiple agencies including health authorities, local education authorities and social service departments

Whilst many schools provide a single service, others offer multiple services, for example respite, day and residential schooling. It is increasingly important that decision-makers understand how each service operates, in particular the resources consumed and the income generated.

Understanding the relationship between the needs of stakeholders and the features of the service will assist in measuring the extent to which stakeholders are likely to feel satisfied and continue using the service.

Important outcomes of customer and service analysis include estimates of future levels of service demand and information to support pricing decisions, resource deployment and service development.

Three separate processes are suggested, focusing on customers, service costs and demand.

**The process for understanding customers**

Within each stakeholder group there may be a range of needs present. Understanding needs can be quite a complicated process, as even within a stakeholder group these can vary significantly. The degree of variation makes it inappropriate to assume, for example, that there is a 'standard' pupil, yet it is unrealistic to consider each one individually. One approach which can be used is to sub-divide each stakeholder group, a process known as segmentation and defined as 'the process of dividing up the total market into sub-markets or niches so that the organisation may better target its services to the market' (Puffitt, 1993).

There are many approaches to segmenting, each of which potentially yields fresh insights regarding the market. In the instance of pupils this might be on the basis of age, distance they live from the school or, if appropriate, their dependency level, etc. Each segment of the market may have very different needs that might or might not be currently satisfied. Need analysis should directly involve the stakeholder group and not depend on the knowledge of service providers. As it is quite common for customers to be unaware of their needs it may be necessary to help them identify and articulate these, thereby empowering them to make proper decisions.

Using school security as an example, the needs of stakeholders might be:
• *Identified need – physical security*
 *Child need:* To feel safe.
 *Parent need:* To know their child is protected from harm arising from children wandering out of school or intruders gaining access.
 *Purchaser need:* To be able to demonstrate that reasonable steps have been taken to discharge their responsibilities in respect of security.

The service offered by the school may include the following security features:
• *Service features – security*
 *Service features*: 24-hour perimeter security, signing-in book, access badges, etc.

The importance of each need and the value of each feature often varies according to the segment.

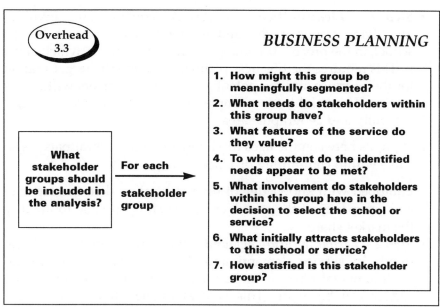

**Figure 3.3** Customer analysis questions

The questions included in Figure 3.3 help develop an understanding of customers and the factors which influence the decision to use the school or service.

**The process for understanding service costs and income**

At this stage it is important to develop an understanding of the costs and income associated with each service. Whilst straightforward in organisations which have only one service or type of activity it can, for many schools and services, be more complex. The following three steps should assist in the process.

- *Step 1 – Identify the total income and expenditure of each service.* Identify for each service the total expenditure, associated income and net cost or surplus. This can be presented on a service-by-service basis, which helps the reader understand the financial impact of each on the performance of the whole organisation. Alternatively it might be worth analysing by expenditure and income by type (staff, premises, etc.).
- *Step 2 – Develop unit costs.* Develop a unit cost for each service which can, with care, be compared with other services or schools, in turn prompting questions about service operation.
- *Step 3 – Extend the analysis.* Within each service, analysis can be extended to provide information on the income and expenditure by customer segment which, for example, can help in understanding the unit cost of different pupil age groups. This might assist in setting age-related fees for each service.

**The process for determining demand**

Business plans require a forecast of activity in order that the overall financial position of the organisation can be estimated. Two steps are involved.

- *Step 1 – Identify trends in service demand.* This involves identifying trends in demand for the services offered by the school, in the process becoming aware of any factors which affect it. This requires the business planner to define the target market for their service and the potential customer numbers within this market. This might, for example, be expressed in terms of age, disability and geographic area:

    'pupils between the ages of 11 and 18 with cerebral palsy who live within commuting distance of the school'.

    Equipped with knowledge of the potential market, the capacity and occupancy of the school or service, it is possible to identify the market share.

- *Step 2 – Estimate future demand.* Taking the current school roll, trends in service demand and the outcomes of the earlier environmental analysis, an estimate of future demand for the service can be made. This is vital to the preparation of the detailed financial projections for the service and should be completed on a term-by-term basis.

**Tips**

1. When selecting a basis for segmentation, focus on characteristics of the customer group and not the service. Examples include age, mobility, purchaser, and distance between home and school.
2. Consider developing service analysis to increase the understanding of features or elements of a service. A school which has a sensory room incurs a level of additional cost. Analysis of the level of use made by different pupil segments would lead to a greater understanding of how this resource is used and the significance of it to different customer segments. Occasionally a feature proves to be unduly expensive given its infrequent use by few pupils. Consideration should be given to switching resources to a feature which yields greater benefits.
3. Keep the analysis simple using graphs, pie charts, etc. to show trends and stress significant points.
4. Where financial data is involved take care regarding the effect of inflation when using data which covers more than one year. Present trends using figures which have been adjusted to remove the effect of inflation.

*Question 5: What do we know about competitors or alternative providers?*

The significance of this element of business planning varies according to the view taken with regard to competition. Some schools and services take the view that they are in competition with each other to attract pupils, and therefore funding, with a result being that they tend to adopt practices commonly seen in business, becoming quite aggressive in the way they market the school. Other services and schools do not hold the view that they are competing, viewing others simply as 'alternative providers'.

Irrespective of the stance taken, understanding how others operate is potentially valuable to all schools and services. For those competing it provides a framework for analysis, thereby developing an understanding of competitors and an approach to marketing the school. For the remainder it provides a framework for 'alternative provider analysis' which can develop into benchmarking.

### The process for competitor analysis

The process for undertaking competitor or alternative provider analysis is similar. This is detailed below, firstly by reference to competitor analysis and then modified for alternative provider analysis.

- *Step 1 – Identifying potential competitors.* Using available knowledge of the market and feedback from parents, purchasers and staff, identify schools or services which appear to be competitors.
- *Step 2 – Filter 'real' competitors.* It is easy to fear that everyone is a competitor, and care needs to be taken to select only those schools or services which pose a real threat. This can be done by considering for each potential competitor whether they operate in the same geographic market, target the same customer segments, and offer similar services. Additionally a consideration might be whether they have attracted or are likely to attract pupils that could have selected your school or service.
- *Step 3 – Gather data.* Having selected the 'real' competitors the next step is to gather data on their financial performance, details of how they operate, services offered, pricing, staff salaries, terms and conditions, reputation, etc. Access to some of this may be difficult, with the main source being published information including their prospectus, advertising material, published accounts, etc. On a wider basis discussions with parents, purchasers, etc. who have visited a number of schools when making a placement decision may well prove to be a good source of information.
- *Step 4 – Analyse data.* This step involves building a picture of the competition by piecing together information gathered from a number of sources. The questions included in Figure 3.4 can help make sense of this data.

Some of these questions are difficult to answer from the available information, which in the early years of business planning will be fragmented, but over time this will improve and quite a full picture can be gained.

- *Step 5 – What can we learn about our own performance?* The information gleaned from the analysis should be used to challenge existing practices. This might lead to reconsideration of earlier parts of the planning process, perhaps causing some strengths and weaknesses to become more or less important. Business planners might also wish to consider changes to existing operations as a

**BUSINESS PLANNING**

**Competitor or Alternative Provider Questions**

1. What services do they offer?
2. Who funds or purchases from them?
3. Where is their market-place?
4. Why do their customers use them?
5. What do we know about them (size, premises, staff base, strengths and weaknesses, performance, reputation, how they operate, prices, etc.)?
6. What appears to be their approach to competition?
7. Is anything known about their future intentions?

**Figure 3.4** Competitor or alternative provider questions

result of this analysis. The learning gained will also help shape the way in which the school is marketed.

• *Step 6 – Selecting a basis for competing.* The final stage in competitor analysis is to consider the basis upon which the school or service should compete in the market-place.

If alternative provider analysis is the preferred approach, the starting point is to select a school or service considered to be of a high standard, either from personal experience or reputation. The analysis then proceeds as with Steps 3, 4, and 5 above.

**Tips**

1. Ensure data-gathering regarding competitors or alternative providers continues throughout the year.
2. Monitor the market constantly to identify possible new competitors.
3. Consider assigning responsibility for monitoring individual competitors to named members of staff.

*Question 6: What do we know about opportunities and threats?*

Opportunities and threats as described by Martin and Smith (1993) are events or trends considered potentially favourable or unfavourable to the organisation. During earlier analysis certain opportunities or threats will have been identified which need to be brought together in a formal process for analysis and possible action.

**The process for analysing opportunities and threats**

This is a straightforward analysis, which can be tackled in the following steps.

- *Step 1 – Initial identification of opportunities and threats.* Review the earlier analysis, in particular SPELT, market and competitor analysis, identifying potential opportunities and threats.

  *Example:* The creation of unitary authorities poses a threat to the school. The relationship with the county council, which is currently good, will in future only relate to four existing pupils. Six existing pupils will now be sponsored by three new unitary authorities. Relationships will need to be quickly built with those responsible for purchasing.

- *Step 2 – Extended identification of opportunities and threats.* Taking the list produced in Step 1, identify any further opportunities or threats which should be considered.

- *Step 3 – Analysis of opportunities and threats.* Consider each identified opportunity or threat and decide whether it should be classified as one which either:

  (a) directly concerns customers and/or services, an example being the development of a respite care scheme; or

  (b) concerns how the school or service is run and indirectly affects customers, an example being the pursuit of Investors in People.

  Both types will need further consideration when identifying objectives.

- *Step 4 – Initial appraisal.* Taking each opportunity or threat in turn, initially appraise it aiming to identify:

  (a) opportunities which appear to have the potential to warrant further investigation;

  (b) threats which if not responded to could pose significant problems for the school.

**Tips**

1. Be prepared for some factors to appear both as an opportunity and a threat.

Having answered the six key questions the analysis stage of the planning process is complete. As a considerable amount of information will have been gathered, analysed and recorded it is advisable to prepare a short summary. This serves two purposes. Firstly, it encourages planners to stand back from the detail and draw out the key points. Secondly, the summary should be included in the plan, as it helps the reader to check their understanding of the position of the school or service, and prepares them for considering direction.

*Completing the analysis section of the business plan*

*Chapter 4*

# Preparing the Business Plan – Setting Direction

### *Introduction*

With the analysis stage complete the attention of business planners should move to determining the direction of the school or service. This stage comprises four elements.

1. Identifying the givens.
2. Determining the mission.
3. Setting objectives.
4. Selecting strategies.

### *Element 1: Identifying the givens*

In most organisations planners have limited freedom, being required to meet the expectations of the main stakeholding group, often senior management, politicians, trustees, etc. In schools, governors may be considered to be the main stakeholder in the presentation and approval of the business plan.

A useful way of thinking of stakeholder requirements is in terms of 'givens' which provide boundaries for the future direction of the school or service.

Identifying the givens helps the business planners to produce a plan which is likely to be acceptable to decision-makers, in the process developing a shared understanding of the parameters within which the school or service operates.

The number and nature of givens varies according to statutory responsibilities, registration, local authority and purchaser requirements. Whilst some of these givens are beyond the control of the decision-makers, others reflect decisions made by them on moral or political grounds. These are referred to as constraints and restraints in *Business Planning for Schools* (Puffitt, Stollen and Winkley, 1992).

In practice head teachers are often aware of the givens, as governors have expressed these in meetings or have made them clear through their actions. For example, during budget approval there may be a united view that 'whatever happens the school must achieve a break-even budget'.

In many cases, however, givens are less explicit and work needs to be undertaken to identify or confirm these.

**The process**

The starting point is for the planning team to identify those givens within which the proposed direction should fit.

*Example:* The pupil/staff ratio must be appropriate to the level of disability.

Having identified the givens, the decision-makers should be asked for their comments, resulting in givens being deleted, changed or added as appropriate.

At the end of this process the business planners will be left with a short list of givens which are clear, agreed and can be included in the business plan.

**Tips**

1. Focus on 'givens' which appear relevant to business planning. Normally these are few in number.
2. Attempt to express and gain agreement of givens in a way which allows the business planning team room for manoeuvre. A given expressed as 'must comply with LEA policy on health and safety' makes an important point but leaves planners freedom over how to comply with it.

Once the givens have been identified, the mission of the school or service can be considered. In the first cycle of business planning it may be necessary to prepare a mission statement, whilst in subsequent years this will either require confirming or changing.

*Element 2: Determining the mission*

The mission statement is an expression of why an organisation exists. In some organisations this is presented in the form of an aim, or purpose statement. Whilst these are different, they each fulfil the need for a simple, clear statement of what the organisation is about.

An example of a mission statement is:

> 'Beaumont seeks to be the national expert college for students with cerebral palsy and associated disabilities whose educational needs cannot be met within their local community.'

**The process**

The following process is suggested.

- *Step 1 – Identify initial themes.* Each member of the management team writes a sentence or paragraph which captures why they think the school or service exists. The outputs of this exercise are shared and discussed, leading to the identification of any common themes.
- *Step 2 – Preparing the draft statement.* Once the common themes are identified, the management team prepares a draft mission

statement for the school or service.
- *Step 3 – Statement testing.* The draft mission statement is tested with a number of stakeholders who are asked:
    (a) to explain what they think it means;
    (b) to consider the extent to which it matches their current view of the school or service;
    (c) for any suggestions for improving the statement.
- *Step 4 – Preparing the final statement.* The final statement should be prepared taking account of the feedback from stakeholders.

If there is an existing mission statement the management team should consider the appropriateness of this to future activities, if necessary preparing a new statement along the lines indicated.

**Tips**

1. Be prepared for this to be a difficult part of the planning process. Often this is the point at which major choices are made. In preparing a mission statement the school or service 'goes public' about why it exists, so a member of staff who believes, for example, that the school should be open to all pupils with disability will disagree with a statement which indicates that the school focuses on children with one particular disability.
2. Avoid the temptation to write a mission statement which accommodates the views of everyone.

Trying to reflect the individual views of each of the business planning team will tend to result in a long and confusing statement. Short, clear statements are normally more effective in conveying why an organisation exists.

## *Element 3: Setting objectives*

Whilst the mission statement states why the organisation exists, the objectives specify what is to be achieved. The Local Government Management Board describes objectives as being 'quantified, measurable performance indicators' (LGMB, 1991). Whilst the mission tends to be stable over a long period of time, objectives tend to change with each business plan.

Objectives make an important contribution to the management of the school, assisting in resource allocation, performance monitoring and future business planning.

Typically organisations have a large number of objectives, some important, others less so. The Local Government Management Board defines two types of objectives: primary objectives 'which have to be achieved if the organisation is to survive, let alone succeed', and secondary objectives which do not carry the same importance. A common weakness of business plans is the inclusion of numerous secondary objectives, or objectives which are primary but are unmeasurable and/or unrealistic.

Some objectives are a constant feature of the business plan, whilst others are included on a temporary basis. Temporary primary objectives often address weakness or opportunities seized.

Examples include:

- *As a constant feature:* 'To achieve the annual budget included in the plan'.
- *On a temporary basis and addressing a weakness:* 'Developing and implementing an IT strategy for the whole school by 30 September 1998'.
- *Responding to a need:* 'Redesigning reception to provide greater security. To be completed by 1 September 1997'.
- *Seizing an opportunity:* 'Introducing a respite scheme in July 1999'.

The objectives to be included in the Business Plan will arise from a number of sources including:

1. The current business plan.
2. The analysis summary which draws together important weaknesses; market, service and competitor information; and opportunities and threats.
3. The givens.

Within the plan the objectives simply state what the organisation is intending to achieve. The means by which this will happen are outlined later in the strategy section.

## The process

The following questions can help determine the objectives which should be included in a business plan.

1. *Is the objective important?* The test of whether an objective is of primary importance is whether failing to achieve it would seriously affect the performance of the school or service.
2. *Can the objective be expressed in measurable terms?* Objectives should be measurable, otherwise it will be difficult to assess whether they have subsequently been achieved.
3. *Is the objective realistic?* Given the track record of the school, resources available and other pressures on management, is the objective realistic.
4. *Does the objective flow from earlier analysis?* Rarely should objectives surprise the reader who, having read the earlier parts of the plan, understands the organisation and environment.
5. *Does the objective 'fit' the givens and mission statement?* If the objective does not fit these the plan is likely to be rejected.

## Tips

1. Avoid writing objectives that are vague and expressed in general terms. For example, an objective which states *'that pupils should have an enjoyable experience'*, whilst laudable, is vague. This can be considered further by asking the question *'How will you know that children find it an enjoyable experience?'*. The answer may be

expressed in different ways, for example lower pupil absence, more children stating they are enjoying school, reduced bullying, etc., each of which can be expressed in a clearer measurable way, for example:

'To reduce the level of pupil absence to x per cent a year.'

'To reduce the instances of bullying to zero by the second year of the business plan.'

'To increase the percentage of pupils stating that they enjoy school by 10 per cent in each of the three years of the business plan.'

## *Element 4: Selecting strategies*

Strategies are the fourth element in the direction section of the plan, without which the school or service is unlikely to achieve the objectives, thus disappointing stakeholders.

The term 'strategy' can be defined in many different ways. The one which describes its role within business planning is:

'a means of achieving a desired end' (Richardson and Richardson, 1992).

*Example:* An example of a strategy related to reducing the level of bullying within school might be to 'undertake a survey of pupils and staff and prepare a report for consideration and action by the management team'.

In this example it would be premature to define the actions for dealing with bullying, and the strategy is therefore concerned with how such actions will be identified.

In many circumstances there are alternative strategies or means to achieving the desired end, and a choice therefore needs to be made.

As strategies are developed the business planner gains a view of the combined implications of pursuing the objectives within the plan. If the implications are excessive, for example demands on staff time, it may be necessary to limit the objectives, change their timing or select different strategies. Usually a combination of strategies is required for the school or service to achieve all its objectives. This can be problematic, as one strategy aimed at meeting an objective might weaken the achievement of others. A decision to establish a sensory room may assist in meeting the objective of improving facilities but adversely impact on the short-term financial objective (unless higher fees can be charged for those who benefit, or higher occupancy results).

**The process**

The following process should lead to the development and selection of strategies which are individually relevant and together achieve all the objectives of the school.

- *Stage 1.* Taking each objective in turn, identify possible strategies for achieving it.

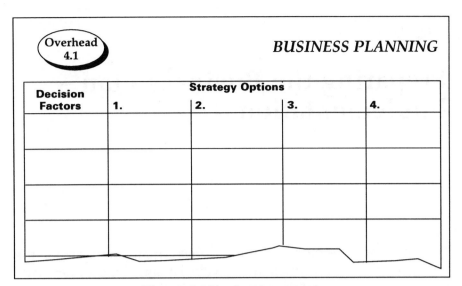

**Figure 4.1** Evaluation matrix

- *Stage 2.* Develop in outline each strategy and check it against the givens, filtering unacceptable strategies and reducing the options for further consideration.
- *Stage 3.* Develop an evaluation matrix as shown in Figure 4.1, with strategic options on the horizontal axis and decision factors on the vertical. There are a considerable number of potential decision factors, including the impact on each of the strengths and weaknesses, the likely achievement of objectives, and financial implications.

  This approach provides a structured way of evaluating options, making them visible to the team and providing an opportunity to test their individual and collective understanding.
- *Stage 4.* Consider which strategies should be adopted, being prepared to go through the cycle of strategy development several times.

**Tips**

At different stages of strategy development those leading the process will need to encourage business planners to be:

1. Divergent in generating strategies.
2. Challenging when looking at existing ways of operating.
3. Open to discussing options fully.
4. Convergent in finally selecting the strategies to be included in the plan.

*Chapter 5*

# Preparing the Business Plan – Implementation

The final main section of the business plan summarises the arrangements for implementation, with the aim being to persuade the decision-maker that the plan can, and will, happen.

When considering this section care needs to be taken to avoid unnecessary detail, and to be clear regarding the actions required, the person responsible and arrangements for monitoring. The reader should believe that the proposed strategies have been thought through, are realistic and will happen. This part of the plan should include:

1. An implementation summary.
2. A financial plan.
3. A contingency plan.

## Implementation summary

Whilst some strategies are simply a continuation of existing practice, others will need new actions to be implemented.

To ensure that the required actions will occur, a 'responsible person' should be identified together with key dates. This allows a picture of the volume and timing of planned activity to emerge, and might cause those planning to question the scheduling of actions and workload of individual staff.

As a final part of this summary the monitoring arrangements should be determined so that the decision-maker understands the arrangements for plan implementation and the frequency with which it will be monitored. Options include routine management team or governors' meetings, and *ad hoc* review meetings with a choice of frequency ranging from weekly through monthly and quarterly to annual.

### The process

The process for preparing the implementation summary is straightforward and can be completed in tabular form, as indicated in Figure 5.1, which uses the example of introducing a staff development programme. This was designed as one of the responses to the objective:

> 'To reduce annual staff turnover by 30 per cent by the end of the second year of the business plan.'

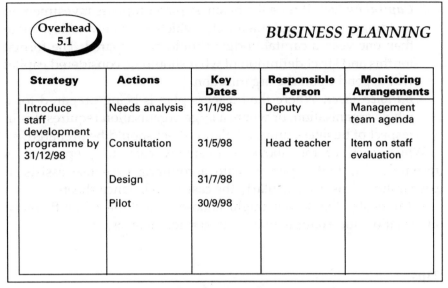

**Figure 5.1** Implementation summary

**Tips**

1. Include only the major actions in the implementation summary.
2. Beware of the head teacher becoming responsible for all strategies. Whilst the head may need to be involved, another member of staff might be a more appropriate choice to ensure actions are complete.

A business plan should include financial statements relating to the plan period. In respect of Year 1 this will primarily be the budget, and in Years 2 and 3 broader financial forecasts.

Financial statements cannot be completed until towards the end of the planning process as they require considerable non-financial and financial detail, including assumptions regarding activity, fees, funding formulas, inflation, staff turnover, depreciation, etc. These assumptions should be explicit, linking to earlier parts of the plan, in particular trends in service demand, environmental factors and strategies proposed for changing or developing the school or service.

The statements included within the financial plan vary depending on the organisation and sector. These include:

1. *Revenue account/budgeted profit and loss account* for the first year and bottom-line forecasts for remaining years. This includes all the income and day-to-day expense budgets of the school or service, with the format following the requirement of the organisation. An example of a revenue account is included as Appendix B.
2. *Cash-flow forecast,* monthly for the first year and quarterly for remaining years. Where the organisation is exposed to the risk of running out of money then a cash-flow forecast is required. This records the movement of money moving in and out of the organisation. A format for a cash-flow forecast is included as Appendix C.

*Financial plan*

37

3. *Capital budget.* Where the business plan proposes investment in buildings, plant, equipment, etc. which are likely to last more than one year, a capital budget should be prepared. The format for this and strict definition of what should be considered capital will depend upon the organisation.
4. *Balance sheet.* Where the business plan is being prepared for a whole organisation, or where a large organisation requires this in respect of business units, a balance sheet should be prepared.

Whilst each of the above is relatively easy to prepare, it is recommended that a person with accounting expertise assists in preparation. This is particularly the case with balance sheets.

Additionally the school might choose to include other financial information, for example unit costs, service analysis, etc.

### Tips

1. Avoid overloading the reader. Include only essential information.
2. Present financial information in a reader-friendly way. This is helped by rounding figures so they are easy to read, using graphs, charts, etc.
3. State any assumptions. For example, demand for the service, inflation, staff turnover, etc.

## Contingency plan

In completing the business plan consideration should be given to the possibility that events might not happen as expected. It is suggested a contingency plan be prepared using the following process.

### The process

- *Step 1* – Identify factors which could impact on the performance of the school or service (e.g. lower funding than expected, inflation, delay in planning permission for a proposed extension).
- *Step 2* – In respect of identified factors, determine the likelihood of occurrence and potential impact. This will lead to an understanding of the risks to which the school or service is exposed.
- *Step 3* – Identify how each risk is to be managed, either by:
  (a) contingency planning, where thought has been given to how potential problems are identified and then dealt with;
  (b) contingencies where financial amounts are held back just in case; or
  (c) transferring the risk elsewhere, by insurance for example.

### Tips

1. As risk often arises from the assumptions that have to be made in business planning, these should be tested for sensitivity.

This can be done simply by assessing the effect that a percentage change in each variable would have on performance, e.g. if staff pay rises by one per cent more than expected, or if activity fell by five per cent, what would be the impact?

Once the processes involved in considering implementation are complete, there should be sufficient information available to write the business plan. Guidance on writing, presentation and approval is included in Chapter 2.

Once approved, the plan should be implemented following the actions proposed in the final section of the document. Finally, performance should be periodically measured, also as defined within the plan.

*Chapter 6*

# The Scope Experience

**Background**

Scope has within its education provision seven schools, a college, an assessment service, advisory service and a network of pre-school provision training parents to work with their young children – 'School for Parents'.

Although the services are vastly different in size, location and methods, they all have a common theme in that they are services for children and young people with cerebral palsy.

The business planning process grew initially from a need to develop an effective management system for the schools, and secondly from a need to provide the purchasers of the schools and services (local education authorities, health authorities and social services) with more detailed and accurate information. This information needed to substantiate that each individual school and service was providing 'value for money' and was demonstrating the efficient use of resource, a further requirement of the OFSTED inspection framework.

A further impact on the schools and services within Scope was both the development and change in provision outside the independent sector. It was important for all the schools and services to re-examine their place in the education system, to revisit their aims and to ensure they fulfilled an identified need rather than compete with or duplicate LEA provision.

The systems of financial management within Scope meant that each head had an annual budget with no provision to carry over money to the next year. This system encouraged heads to spend up to the maximum of their budget, and did not necessarily lead to an improvement in the quality of teaching and learning.

**The business planning process**

The process started with a group briefing meeting at which the schools and services openly discussed the way they had traditionally been run and the way in which they were currently run. Many of the schools had already prepared and were implementing a school development plan. However, the prevalent pace of educational change forced continual review and revision of what were in effect short-term curriculum plans.

Many of the school development plans in existence were for

internal school or service use only. It was agreed that by working on the business plans, as a group of heads, a more effective, consistent and united system could be produced. It was also agreed that working together would ensure that the process would be set in a context of much greater discipline (an agreed framework and time-scale) and a more open and sharing attitude would be fostered.

It was agreed that one of the business plans would be used as a 'live case model' to enable others to follow and learn from the experience. A time-scale was set to ensure that plans were well in advance of the budget cycle (a 1 April start to the financial year), and that by December the plans would be complete and fully costed prior to information on the budget being given to the schools in February (Figure 6.1).

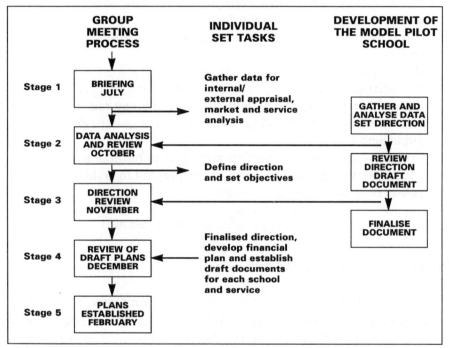

**Figure 6.1** The Scope process

In this exercise the pilot school developed its business plan through the agreed process but one step ahead of the rest of the group. This school fed each section of its work into the whole group meetings at Stages 2, 3, and 4. This meant that there was always a practical example to work with and learn from.

**Stage 1: The group briefing meeting**

At the briefing meeting the schools and services decided upon an overarching statement to describe the overall aim and philosophy for the education provision, and also established a set of practical steps which each individual service intended to take in order to come close to fulfilling this mission. The first part of this exercise, describing an ideal, was extremely pleasurable to do but the second part, that of identifying and ensuring practical steps to achieve this ideal, was a little more difficult. However, it proved to be very productive, resulting in the service aim (Figure 6.2).

---

**The aim of Education Services is to ensure 'a quality education through the empowerment of all' achieved through:**

- Working with those with cerebral palsy, parents and carers to identify and secure the most appropriate means of meeting their educational needs.
- Working with local groups, other educational providers and voluntary organisations.
- Collaborating with schools, colleges, LEAs, social service departments and health authorities in developing a comprehensive and accessible range of quality education services.
- Working with advisory bodies for the full recognition of the educational needs and rights of those with cerebral palsy.
- Campaigning on legislation and disability, thereby raising awareness in the community; commissioning, undertaking and publishing research.
- Undertaking writing for journals and other publications on education, therapy and care issues with regard to children and young people with cerebral palsy.

---

**Figure 6.2** Scope education services aim

### Stage 2: Data analysis and review

Each school and service examined their own provision by initially undertaking an internal appraisal identifying the strengths and weaknesses of their organisation as they perceived them. Many schools undertook this analysis with their senior management teams, and others used a combination of staff and governors (including parent governors).

This was followed by an appraisal of the external factors affecting the services (SPELT – see Chapter 3), which highlighted many developments or changes in the environment which were often beyond the school's control but none the less impacted on the school or service. Examples of this were as follows.

- *Sociological* – 'The evolution of integration and the expectation of inclusive education had lead to special schools needing to ensure that integration is an essential part of their philosophy, and have also demanded that they develop new skills in the key areas of advisory work and outreach services.'
- *Political* – 'The level of government funding to local authorities is less likely to enable the authorities to fund "out-county" placements.'
- *Economic* – 'The financial demands being made upon local

authorities have led independent schools to do far more detailed financial work to enable the authorities to support them. Each fee charged has to be completely broken down to enable the composition to be fully understood and justified, and fees need to be broken down into their component local authority parts to enable the lead authority, normally the education authority, to "charge-on" the relevant health or social service component parts.'

- *Legal* – 'EEC regulations are now starting to impact significantly in regards to business planning, whether on working hours for residential staff, personnel regulations, or demanding health and safety regulations.'
- *Technological* – 'The impact of early medical intervention has lead to children coming into schools with far more complex disabilities and in many cases including a sensory impairment.'

This part of the process stimulated the most debate and gave a view of the school in the wider environment. Where there was an accurate view of the external environment, e.g. the requirements of the Children Act and residential schools, it was possible to identify clearly the potential impact. Where there was less certainty, planning needed to take account of far more alternative scenarios.

Each school and service was also asked to look at a school or service similar to themselves and to compare costs, staffing levels, pupil roll, etc. This useful comparative study was a first step towards introducing benchmarking and gaining an understanding of alternative providers. As a result schools had a sound basis for questioning their own performance and a better understanding of which alternative provision might pose a threat in the future.

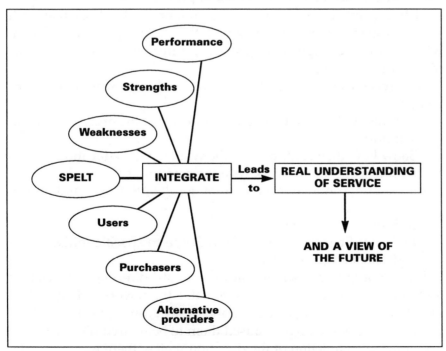

**Figure 6.3** Data analysis and interpretation

Further detailed analysis documenting the 'customers' of each school and service identified that, whilst professionals were the main purchasers, the plan needed to recognise the needs of parents and pupils.

Opportunities and threats arising from the internal and external analysis were also detailed, and all the data gathered was integrated into a simple summary (Figure 6.3). This summary of the analysis highlighted the current picture of each school or service. Previous 'crystal ball gazing' that many schools resorted to when writing their development plans was replaced with sound and substantial information with a detailed assessment of the environment and the market-place.

**Stage 3: Direction review**

The next part of the process was for each school and service to establish their own individual mission or aims statement, and to outline clear objectives and strategies to achieve this. In this process they addressed any issues which had arisen from the analysis.

To integrate the school's development plans into this process some of the heads identified as an objective 'to achieve the school development plan'. Other schools identified a particular proposal within their plan which they viewed as being crucial to the future of the school or service. It was important that each objective could be easily measurable, and clearly linked to developing the strengths of the school, remedying weakness, and exploiting opportunities for meeting the aims. This linkage improved the persuasiveness of the plan and increased the likelihood of approval.

At this point in the process it was important to check that each school's direction was in keeping with the wider organisation, falling within a set of management 'givens', and furthering the wider goals of the organisation.

The givens were identified as follows, with each school or service being required to:
- Comply with legislation and the policies of the organisation and statutory bodies.
- Show how they contribute to the whole of the education service within Scope and to work with the community.
- Maximise contract income from local authorities and health authorities.
- Include a financial target.
- Link any financial subsidy from Scope to specific initiatives or additional levels of service.

This set of givens ensured that the schools' direction was realistic and set in a consistent and systematic framework. Many initial objectives were more like 'dreams and desires', and considering them in the context of the givens caused them to be revised (Figure 6.4).

Following completion of the direction review there were two vital processes, developing the financial plan and writing the overall plan.

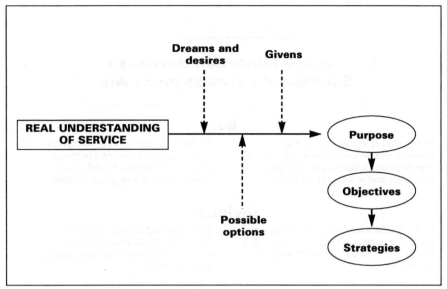

**Figure 6.4** Developing direction

**Financial plan**

The objectives and strategies identified by the schools and services needed to be set in the context of a clear financial plan. This plan was to include all the income and expenditure associated with running the school or service for the period of the plan. The first year of the plan had to have the detail needed for the annual budget, but the remaining years could be in less detail. At this stage of the process many heads developed their financial plans by analysing their objectives and focusing on what was to be achieved rather than on how money had traditionally been spent.

**Writing the plan**

In many cases the writing of the plan was the most difficult part of the process. Most heads decided to write the plan themselves although a few utilised the skills of members of their governing body.

At the initial group briefing meeting the heads established the characteristics of a successful business plan, which in effect became the criteria against which their plans would be judged.

Figure 6.5 indicates the criteria which were agreed at the briefing held in July.

*Summary*

Once the process had been established, heads and heads of service began to see the link between financial decisions and the effectiveness of their schools.

In the first year of business planning it was clear that the schools and services did not have access to sufficient detailed data to enable them to make real comparisons of costs between themselves and alternative providers.

---

### Scope Education Services – Successful business plans will

#### Be:

PERSUASIVE (Leading the reader through the document step by step so that planned actions appear logical, desirable and worthy of support)

REALISTIC (Achievable within the likely available resources and within a realistic timetable. Based upon reasonable, stated assumptions)

#### Include:

CUSTOMER ANALYSIS (Showing who currently uses/does not use the service, their pattern of use and motivation to consume)

CONSIDERATION OF THE WIDER ENVIRONMENT (Plan considers possible impact of changes in the wider environment)

A SENSE OF PURPOSE AND MEASURABLE OBJECTIVES (Convey why the business unit exists and what it will achieve. This will be communicated in a clear and passionate way)

STRATEGIES/ACTIONS (Clear means by which objectives are to be achieved. These should play to the strengths, remedy weaknesses and be consistent with the assessment of the environment and market-place)

COSTINGS (Clear summary of the financial implications of the plan)

### Scope Education Services – Successful business plans will

SHOW THAT AN APPROPRIATE PROCESS HAS BEEN USED (Wider knowledge and expertise within the unit has been used in an appropriately consultative and participative way, and the plan has the commitment of all staff)

FIT WIDER ORGANISATIONAL MISSION AND GIVENS (Immediately apparent how the unit furthers the goals of the organisation)

FEEL ACCURATE (Include appropriate numerical data together with stated assumptions and an assessment of sensitivity)

BE APPROPRIATE (Convey sufficient information to be persuasive without inviting the reader to engage in debate over detail)

BE PRODUCED ON TIME (To meet institutional deadlines and allow proper discussion)

BE WRITTEN FOR THE AUDIENCE (The level of explanation, language used and emphasis given will reflect the needs of the intended reader)

BE APPROPRIATELY RADICAL/CONSERVATIVE
(Radical changes which are often brave and inherently risky may be essential. Conservative approaches might feel safe but could be shortsighted and inappropriate)

**Figure 6.5** Characteristics of a successful business plan

This data collection was built into the time-scale for the next year's business planning process, and key cost headings in different schools were selected for comparison on expenditure. Encouraging a more open and honest approach to school and service budgeting was a positive element of the whole process.

In future years this process could be further enhanced and developed, with additional analysis of cost headings and a detailed investigation of the impact that these costs have upon the efficiency of the units. By gaining an insight into the expenditure of other schools, and analysing the impact of the specific budget decisions of other colleagues, schools and services could further examine and review their own expenditure and question decisions that may have been made previously.

The exercise was of considerable value both to individual head teachers and to the heads of service, as well as contributing to the cohesiveness of the whole group. It is an exercise which would be of enormous value to special school head teachers across the country whether on a whole organisation, local authority, area or cluster basis.

# Chapter 7

# Example Business Plan – Meldreth Manor School

This chapter focuses on the business plan for Meldreth Manor, one of seven schools run by Scope. This example has been selected because of the size and complexity of provision. Meldreth Manor School was the pilot school when business planning was introduced within Scope. The plan included within this chapter is a clear improvement on that generated in the first year, having benefited from the evaluation and feedback process.

This chapter includes:

1. Introductory comments to guide readers as they read the plan for Meldreth Manor School.
2. The business plan, which covers a four-year period.
3. Observations by the head teacher regarding the experience of business planning.

*Introductory comments*

The business plan which follows is that written for consideration by Scope management. This has been subject to some editing at the request of Scope owing to the confidential nature of the content. In particular:

1. The content within the section on competitor (alternative provider) analysis has been edited to remove reference to other schools.
2. All financial data has been deleted, as has the contingency plan.

The plan format follows that advocated in Chapter 2, and in quality terms is typical of what should be achievable in the second round of business planning.

This plan was submitted to the Director of Contract Services within Scope. In addition, as part of the commitment to improving the quality of planning processes within the school, the document has been subject to a technical evaluation using the form included as Appendix D. Owing to confidentiality the content of this evaluation has not been included, but is generally positive and recommends the development of further planning tools for the next cycle. In particular these will be aimed at increasing information available regarding customer segments and services.

# Meldreth Manor School
# Business Plan

This plan for Meldreth Manor School offers a detailed one-year plan within the broad framework of development for the next three years.

Within Scope there are clear priorities within which this plan must operate. These provide the givens for the establishment of this plan.

- To ensure that Scope is financially healthy.
- To ensure that people with cerebral palsy are empowered in Scope and the external world.
- To improve working relationships with Local Groups. [Local Groups are Scope's network of small independent charities].
- To review and develop existing and new services and activities which address identified need.
- To promote Scope externally.
- To achieve consistent and systematic management.

## 1.0 Introduction

Meldreth Manor School is one of the premier residential schools for pupils with cerebral palsy and severe or profound and multiple learning difficulties in the UK. The school currently takes pupils from throughout the UK, although the greater numbers of pupils come from the South-east and the Midlands. In addition the school has begun to attract interest from parents of children born overseas and from parents currently serving in the armed forces.

### Mission

The school mission is:

'Putting Pupils First – We exist as a school to enable the individual to gain in self-esteem and autonomy through an understanding of their abilities and potential as a person.'

The school is set in six acres of grounds in rural Cambridgeshire and caters for just under 100 young people a year. The school offers an integrated curriculum model in which members of a multidisciplinary team work as a unit to deliver all aspects of provision to children and young adults aged between six and 21 consistently across the full 24 hours. This includes a 'Total Communication' approach.

The school is divided into four working units, each with their own staff team and management structure. Each unit works within the policy and procedures laid down across the whole school. The school operates within a statutory framework incorporating both the Children Act 1989 and the SEN Code of Practice 1993; in addition the school complies fully with the policy and procures laid down by the Executive Council of Scope.

The school operates for 38 weeks a year, divided into three terms. Additionally, the school offers a holiday respite scheme during the summer. This is funded separately from the provision of the main school.

The school has a commitment to full access and progression within the National Curriculum, and couples this with a vision of the whole curriculum for people with complex needs.

The reputation of the school as an example of best practice and as an innovative centre has been firmly established during the past year with a series of articles in the national press, including *The Independent, The Times* and *The Times Educational Supplement*.

Over the past year and during the preceding three years, analysis of the pupil base at the school establishes that there has been a marked increase in pupil numbers from 85 to 95. In addition the range of needs that the school has sought to meet has both diversified and increasingly included young people with more complex needs, as represented by the increase in pupils with bi-partite and tri-partite funding (LEA and social services, or LEA, social services and health authority).

# 2.0 Analysis

## 2.1 Performance appraisal

### *Review of previous business plan objectives*

The current business plan includes nine objectives detailed below, together with details of the current level of achievement.

Meldreth Manor School is committed to constant improving standards whilst maximising and increasing disposable income.

To achieve this we will:

*Finance*

1. Ensure that the budget submission for the year has a zero deficit prior to reallocation of central costs by Scope.
   **Achieved.** Financial target for the year was a zero deficit; in practice the school should achieve a contribution towards overheads of £X.
2. Increase voluntary income by X per cent over the previous year's baseline.
   **Achieved.** Last year the school had other income of £X. This year the school has achieved other income of £X, an increase of approximately 20 per cent. This did not include £X of additional income raised by companies and trusts against expenditure in budget at Meldreth Manor School.
3. Complete a cost reallocation exercise to determine the total cost of each pupil placement in the school by September.
   Considerable progress has been made towards this objective, software to allow analysis has been purchased and training undertaken. This objective will be completed by the end of the next financial year.

*Curriculum*

4. Implement SAT assessments linked to teacher-led assessment with pupils at all key stages by June.
   **Achieved.**

5. Trial the use of complementary therapies with six named pupils in the further education (FE) unit from April, to determine whether such approaches enhance learning.

   **Achieved** and further development agreed. The initial trial of the use of aromatherapy during the spring demonstrated a need for further focused research. A training programme to support the work has been planned for implementation in January.

6. Produce and implement a curriculum development plan.

   **Achieved.** Appropriate time and resources led to increased understanding of roles from curriculum co-ordinators, who developed skills of planning and budgeting to support the annual cycle and to develop a clear plan of resourcing the curriculum over the coming three years.

*Buildings and grounds*

7. Prepare and agree a major expenditure plan (MEP) to develop the FE unit in light of inspection reports and DfEE and FEFC guidance, for the planned budget.

   **Achieved and submitted.** The MEP was prepared and agreed in principle with the Director of Contract Services. The budget contained the professional fees for the coming year and these were invested in the early part of the year. Final agreement to begin building work was given at the end of March.

*Staff development*

8. Ensure that each member of child contact staff is released for one day during the year to explore strengths of other provision and services.

   **Partially achieved:** 22 teachers, nurses, therapists and managers took advantage of this scheme. The information gleaned contributed to the development of the plan.

9. Establish a programme of management development linked to core competencies for all managers by September.

   **Established and reviewed.** A programme of development was drawn up in conjunction with an external consultant. A review of the programme was called for November; this review indicated a need for external validation of any programme, so the programme was then reduced during the spring to focus upon training in personnel procedures.

### Review of financial performance

The past six years have seen concerted growth in pupil numbers, which have risen from 80 to 97 in the current year. Simultaneously we have achieved rises in fee income of X per cent. In the last year this has included real increases in fees of X per cent above inflation with an acceptance of the fee strategy by purchasers.

Throughout these past three years expenditure has been carefully controlled. Staffing costs have risen by only X per cent, despite the X per cent increase in pupil numbers. Although in the past the growth in pupil numbers has been assimilated due to spare capacity we have now reached the point at which we are operating at full capacity and staff are already working to their limits to achieve the standards expected.

Property maintenance has been sustained in line with a five-year rolling programme of development in the light of statutory requirements. This has allowed the school to retain a quality site and to make significant improvements to facilities and the general state of repair. However, the large six-acre site continues to require high levels of investment to maintain the state of repair.

Equipment purchases have grown significantly during the past three years. This reflects planned and budgeted expenditure upon resources to support the success of the 24-hour curriculum model. During the review period we can observe increased expenditure of around £X. This has been facilitated by increased expenditure on resources through which pupils can learn without constantly requiring staff supervision and involvement. This supports the mission of the school in seeking to promote pupil autonomy and also supports cost-effective techniques of promoting learning across the whole curriculum. The areas in which the school has established its reputation and unique selling points include IT and communication. It must be noted that such areas are constantly updated in the light of technological innovation, and hence require increased expenditure.

Meldreth Manor School has demonstrated great success in establishing itself as a market leader, with high standards of financial control where small surpluses are used to promote pupil learning and enhance the environment to allow for growth in the future. This position recognises that there have been no attempts for performance measures to include the reallocation of central costs, or the contribution made to the wider organisation (Scope) by staff at the school. The financial position therefore reflects the model defining surplus and deficit established by Scope in 1993, and it is likely that more sensitive measures of financial performance will be introduced during the next two years.

The year saw continued growth to the total income of the school and simultaneously the steady development of a process of devolution of expenditure throughout the school. The surplus of operational income over expenditure has allowed the school to move towards making a real contribution toward Scope to support operational overheads. This is reflected in the chart (Figure 7.1).

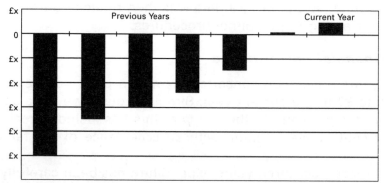

**Fig. 7.1** Moving towards a greater contribution to Scope

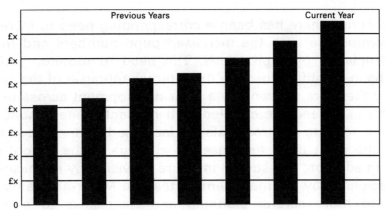

**Fig. 7.2** Fee income analysis

Analysis of income during the same period shows marked growth in fee income both as a result of increased pupil numbers and the successful negotiation of fee increases that seek to recover the total cost of placement (Figure 7.2).

This has been accompanied by growth in other income to the school through the summer respite scheme, which has been reviewed and found to be increasingly cost-effective. This also allows greater access to the total number of families supported (Figures 7.3 and 7.4).

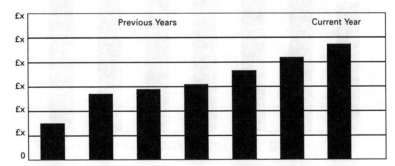

**Fig. 7.3** Other income trend analysis respite scheme and other income

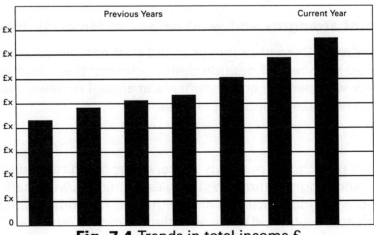

**Fig. 7.4** Trends in total income £

During this period there has been a corresponding need to increase staffing costs to accommodate both the increased pupil numbers and moreover the increased complexity of pupil needs. The need to monitor and rationalise staffing has been identified through the internal appraisal of the school.

In summary therefore we can see a clear development across the years of a steady growth in fee income coupled with prudent management in both the short and long term to control costs by increased financial controls. This is validated by the audit team responses to analysis of the school income and expenditure. In addition, investment in future provision by increasing resources across all disciplines by the management team at Meldreth Manor School has been linked to more careful planning and clear links to a whole-school development plan. The growth of expenditure therefore sees a sustained and controlled increase to accommodate additional pupils with increasingly complex needs (Figure 7.5)

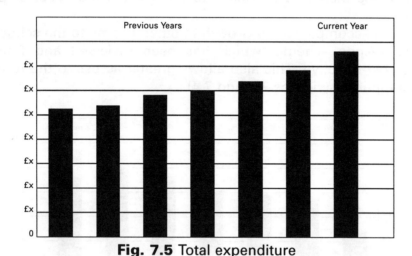

**Fig. 7.5** Total expenditure

## 2.2 Analysis of strengths and weaknesses at Meldreth Manor School

During September to December this year 163 staff completed surveys either as individuals or as members of multidisciplinary teams; the school also reviewed correspondence with parents and comments at annual reviews, and placements by purchasers and stakeholders in placement.

### *Strengths*

The strengths of the school are widely perceived as being related to the ability of pupils to learn and progress through strong relationships with staff. This success was supported with good facilities and with time for staff to study aspects of provision in greater depth, and to show initiative and try out new ideas.

Particular aspects of provision, including IT and communication, were identified as strengths. Purchasers especially noted these.

The importance of multidisciplinary working and of teamwork was repeatedly mentioned, as was the training programme to support this. These strengths were validated in the report of the FEFC inspection team of November. The impact of the training programme for child contact staff was also recognised and applauded in the report of the Investors in People (IIP) assessment team.

A social service inspection in the summer suggested that the practice of support to pupils was of a high standard.

### *Weaknesses*

The success of the school has been achieved at a great cost to individual members of the staff team. The needs of pupils have become more complex and the demands upon staff time have become ever greater. A common theme amongst staff teams was a plea for a reduction in the complexity of school life, simpler communication, less paperwork and hence the criteria of more time to spend on what we do well. These themes were noted in the report of the FEFC team, where it was noted that the changes initiated by the school in September would alleviate these pressures and provide the service with a firm base to continue to develop.

The provision of development opportunities for non-child contact staff was noted as an area requiring further investigation by the IIP assessment.

The school has an overly complex management structure which inhibits managers from making clear and consistent decisions, and has slowed down the ability of individual managers to plan and budget effectively.

Communication within the school has been overly reliant upon the use of meetings, and there is a clear need to dispense with repetition and encourage people to take responsibility. The size of the school makes change hard if consultation takes place with all team members.

Higher than anticipated staff absenteeism was recognised as an important concern throughout the year.

In addition it has been noted that the failure to pay market rates of pay to professional staff, coupled with an increasing scarcity of professionals with appropriate qualifications and experience, could leave the school in a weaker position in the future if action is not taken.

### 2.3 External appraisal (SPELT)

During the past year there have been a number of factors that have been discussed at length in considering the direction of the school. A summary of these is included as Appendix A, and the key points outlined below:
- There have been significant changes to the framework of social service legislation and guidance, most notably the introduction of the 'Looking after Children' framework for placement agreements and review of placement by social services.
- There has been increased pressure to reconsider and revise the school approach to child protection. This has best been recognised in the William

Utting review of the child protection procedures and the advice on recruitment and selection of staff produced in the Warner Report.

- There is increased recognition by local authorities of the need for a diversity of services to be provided to meet the needs of children whose needs cannot be met within the boundaries of local authority provision. This is reflected in the decisions of the Special Educational Needs (SEN) Tribunal.

- The introduction of consortial-based purchasing may mean that there is a significant increase in the purchasing power of large blocks of local authorities.

- A number of authorities have indicated an intention to reduce the total number of services in which they place children to ensure that a closer partnership between schools and authority is maintained.

- There remains a standing problem of recruitment to professional posts whilst Scope continues to pay at below market rates. Whilst this impact has been especially acute in the recruitment and retention of physiotherapists, there have been additional problems in retaining support workers due to the low pay.

- When recruiting teachers the school has also been faced with a difficulty in recruiting those with appropriate qualifications and experience. It has been agreed, therefore, that the school makes better use of school-based professional qualifications initiated by the Teacher Training Agency to train individual support workers as teachers whilst in post.

- Recent decisions in the High Court may allow more authorities to move towards closing a statement of educational needs at the age of 16 and then allowing placement to become the responsibility of the FEFC and social services.

- There have been rapid advances in available technology; the entry-level PC base has now moved from 66MHz machines to 100MHz Pentiums; although prices have dropped there is an increasingly short life-span for technology.

## 2.4 Customer and service analysis

During the year there was continued growth in pupil numbers at Meldreth Manor School, and the purchasing base continued to diversify with a total of 56 purchasers currently making use of the services available from the core business of the school. Most importantly, the major purchaser for the school agreed the planned fee uplift for the coming three years and made clear reference to the continued use of the school as a preferred provider.

A number of referrals were made to the school from 'X' School. The school, which had previously been noted as a competitor, appears to be focusing on making provision for pupils with extremely profound and multiple learning difficulties. This has encouraged more able, older pupils to transfer to Meldreth Manor and the process of transfer has attracted parents of younger pupils at the school. This has also allowed authorities that previously had not been purchasers at Meldreth to make use of our provision for the first time.

For the purpose of this business plan the description of customers will incorporate an analysis of purchasers, the pupil base at the school and the level of dependency in the pupil roll.

During the year the total number of pupils at the school rose to 97, including students aged between 19 and 21 who are not part of the school roll. With the current level of adaptations and with the current high dependency of the pupils on roll this meant that the school was operating at full capacity. The school has the potential for 15 leavers in July, and currently has six places filled. Experience over the past three years has shown that between seven and nine pupils will actually leave in July and that there are currently sufficient pupils seeking places to maintain the school at capacity. An analysis of the demographics of school-leavers for the first two years of the business plan demonstrates a similar trend, with ten potential leavers in Year 1 and 11 in Year 2. Continued marketing will be required to maintain the pupil roll, as will good relationships with purchasers.

During the year there was an increase in the diversity of the customer base for Meldreth Manor School. This was due to new authorities placing pupils in three instances, and increasingly the arrival of bipartite and tripartite funding arrangements. There was continued interest from our major purchasers, and the largest of these noted that we were a preferred provider.

A number of arrivals at the school were due to the tribunal process. During the year the school was involved in five tribunals and the parents won four of these, and the authority placed a pupil at the school. In one case the tribunal found in favour of the authority, although the parents intend to challenge the statement in the future.

Interest and placement were also found from overseas, with the government in 'Y' placing and planning to fund two young men at the school during the coming year. The school also gained in numbers due to the planned change in role for 'X' School, which led to four pupils transferring to Meldreth Manor.

In the year the school noted a general trend towards increasing complexity of need as being the norm for the school in the future. Closer examination of the placements and referrals to the school during the year has confirmed this trend, but that the trend has not been as acute as originally envisaged. The school has recruited pupils with a diversity of need, and there have continued to be placements of young people who are less dependent, and those with greater cognitive and language skills. This increased diversity has assisted the school in providing appropriate peer groups to a wider range of pupils at the school, and hence the school is more attractive to purchasers.

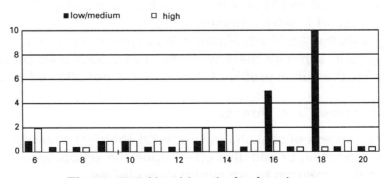

**Figure 7.6** Need level of referral

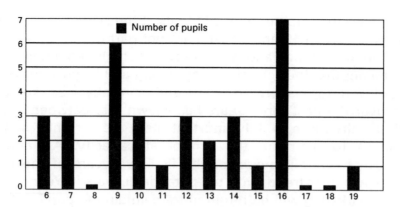

**Figure 7.7** Age spread of referrals 1996/97

The range of need being referred to the school is represented in Figure 7.6.

This demonstrates that there is a clear peak of pupils with a lower dependency likely to attend the school in the FE unit, and a general spread of pupils with varied levels of dependency across the whole school (Figure 7.7).

This demonstrates a trend compared with the current year towards special interest in taking up places at the school during the primary years and at the end of compulsory school-leaving age. It suggests therefore that the first and FE units are likely to have increased levels of interest in the coming year.

## 2.5 Competitor analysis

During the past two years four major competitors have been identified as:
'W' School
'X' School
'Y' School
'Z' School.

Available information regarding these is included in Figure 7.8 together with comparative information in respect of Meldreth Manor School.

Analysis of the business plan and prospectus for each of these services reflects a continued growth in provision for pupils with more complex needs similar to those whose needs are met at Meldreth Manor. However, 'W' and 'X' Schools are operating at capacity and are unlikely to be able to make continued growth over the coming 12 months. 'Y' School is making little impact upon the purchasing base of Meldreth Manor.

This suggests that Meldreth Manor can continue to maintain the pupil roll for the coming year, although there will need to be continued press and PR work to ensure that the public profile of the school is not allowed to slip.

## 2.6 Opportunities and threats

Through the process of consultation with stakeholders a number of areas which could have a positive or negative effect upon the school were identified.

The key points referred to are summarised below.

**Figure 7.8**

| | Meldreth | 'W' School | 'X' School | 'Y' School | 'Z' School | Comments |
|---|---|---|---|---|---|---|
| Status | Independent | | | | | |
| Sector | | Primary | Secondary | Secondary | Primary | |
| Service | 5–19 mixed residential school with small FEFC provision for 19+ | | | | | |
| Size | 90 | | | | | |
| Staff | Integrated staffing drawn from community | | | | | |
| Reputation | Good, highlighted through NFER, SCAA, etc. | | | | | |
| Fees | Full board £X for 38 weeks | | | | | |
| Market share | Major role in pupils with PMLD | | | | | |
| Marketing | Initially through face-to-face contact. Professional prospectus. School substantially networked | | | | | |
| Purchasers | Tri-partite funding possible and increasing. See customer analysis for detail | | | | | |
| Strengths | See SWOT | | | | | |
| Weaknesses | See SWOT | | | | | |

### *Opportunities*

- *Development of Meldreth Manor as an assessment centre and training base.* The school has developed strong links with the Cambridge Institute of Education as a centre from which training can be offered. This could be extended within special education, and moreover throughout Scope.
- *Development of community integration links.* The school has a number of facilities on site that could be more widely offered to those living locally, in the same model as that developed by staff within the indoor riding school. Particular areas noted were the learning curves, hydrotherapy pool and Brunel active balance system equipment.
- *Early years links.* Residential assessments for parents and young children in partnership with the assessment and advisory service could be offered if capacity allowed in the future.
- *Joint ventures with outside agencies.* Three possible joint ventures were identified.
  1. Links with NCET to promote IT provision in special education.
  2. Links with adult services to provide support to local adult services being established.
  3. Links with colleagues working overseas to introduce a European dimension to the work carried out.

### *Threats*

- Development of increased culture of child protection and movement towards a non-educational ethos within residential schooling. Events in residential schools and homes throughout the early part of the year created a difficult culture in which to operate. The need to retain the focus of provision upon education and learning has been discussed with governors at the school.
- Possible shifting of responsibility for funding post-16 education to the FEFC, allowing authorities to allow statements to lapse at the age of 16. This will require careful monitoring throughout next year.
- Difficulties in recruiting sufficient trained teachers to special education more widely may make those we recruit and train more in demand by the public sector paying enhanced wages. A broader platform of benefits for staff working at the school must be established. This should include professional development and public profile.

  In exploring issues relating to the needs of customers we have recognised that purchasing authorities wish to develop closer relationships with a smaller number of non-county providers; close links with contracts teams will need to be maintained and enhanced.

### 2.7 Summary of analysis

The key aspects of the school curriculum have undergone substantial development during the year. Teachers have had extended periods covered to allow for the development of curriculum expertise and assessment, and recording developments. These must be maintained if the school is to have a high-quality response to the planned OFSTED inspection during next year. Particular care will need to be taken to ensure that the curriculum for pupils aged 16 and above allows for high expectations, and furthermore that it supports the needs of pupils with a lower index of dependency.

Throughout the analysis a continued commitment to the curriculum philosophy of the school was evidenced, and the school remains committed to the 24-hour curriculum model and staffing model that is related.

The strengths of the school can then be summarised as:

- 24-hour curriculum and staffing model.
- High levels of expertise and the interdisciplinary approach.
- Excellent facilities with innovative aspects.
- Good relationships with purchasers and media.
- Growing reputation as training centre.

Weaknesses of the school can be seen as:

- Changing expectations of standards of care.
- Overly complex management structure.
- Too many demands being placed upon staff outside of their areas of expertise.

In the analysis of the strengths and weaknesses of the school, taking into account the internal and external appraisal, two key priorities for development were identified:

- Management structures and practice.
- Standards of care.

The school business plan is therefore focused upon the achievement of continued growth in curriculum whilst a thorough review and change in practice occurs in the priority areas. This needs to be linked to an overall plan for development leading to Year 3 of the planning period.

To remain successful the school needs to develop a longer-term three-year strategic view of the process of development. During the coming three-year period the school must seek to continue and consolidate the work completed over the past three years, by continuing to apply the mission and broad aims of the school. In addition the school must seek to continue growth and address the following issues.

- Increased resources for all areas of the whole curriculum.
- Higher levels of competent consistent management at all levels, with greater degrees of responsibility and the authority to take decisions.
- Higher levels of training and development to enhance professional skills and to ensure that best practice is benchmarked against external forces.
- An increased level of financial surplus that can invested in better staffing resources.
- The highest possible standards of care, with full regard to the outcomes of the Utting Review and Warner Report.

## 3.0 Direction

The direction contained in this section reflects the earlier analysis and the givens for schools within this.

### 3.1 Givens

- To ensure that Scope is financially healthy.
- To ensure that people with cerebral palsy are empowered in Scope and the external world.
- To improve working relationships with Local Groups.
- To review and develop existing and new services and activities which address identified need.
- To promote Scope externally.
- To achieve consistent and systematic management.

### 3.2 Mission

This continues to be:

'Putting Pupils First – We exist as a school to enable the individual to gain in self-esteem and autonomy, through an understanding of their abilities and potential as a person.'

### 3.3 Objectives

To fulfil the mission the school has identified a number of primary objectives for the coming year.

1. To implement an agreed management and staffing structure to meet the needs of all staff, supporting pupils by September (Year 1). The management structure should be:
   - Cost-effective.
   - Clear.
   - Cohesive.
   - Supportive of the principles of the 24-hour curriculum.
2. To generate a financial position of a contribution towards overheads of £X per annum.
3. To complete a full cost analysis of pupil placement, completing the objective deferred from the current plan.
4. To raise standards of care in line with school-generated, agreed and common standards across the 24 hours, with full regard to the external environment as demonstrated by the Utting and Warner Reports.
5. To complete implementation of the curriculum development plan. As identified in the current plan.
6. To achieve a FEFC grade of 2 upon re-inspection, ensuring the continued provision of the course (Year 1 of the business plan).
7. To review the training programme and achieve the national standard of Investors in People.

### 3.4 Strategies

- Gain the necessary approval within Scope for the planned new structure, fill the posts and launch the new staffing structure by September. (Objective 1)
- Introduce new prices and other changes arising from the business plan;

continue existing operation. Undertake budget monitoring with particular emphasis on generating additional income. (Objective 2)

- Complete full cost analysis. (Objective 3)
- Develop Standards of Care Statements and identify standards as a key responsibility of new unit manager posts. (Objective 4)
- Release two co-ordinators on a part-time basis to assist in the identification of a new model for curriculum coverage for the 14–19 age group. (Objective 5)
- During the period April to June (Year 1) implement the changes already identified as being necessary to achieve FEFC Grade 2. (Objective 6)
- Review existing training programmes and develop so that these reflect the current needs of individual staff and the business plan. (Objective 7)

# 4.0 Implementation

| Strategy | Dates | Responsibility | Action Plan | |
|---|---|---|---|---|
| Gain the necessary approval within Scope for the planned new structure, fill the posts and launch the new staffing structure by September. (Objective 1) | September | David Banes | March | – Plans to Director of Contract Services for approval |
| | | | April | – Papers to personnel panel for approval |
| | | | May 1 | – Establish development centres for all staff involved in scheme |
| | | | June 1 | – Serve any redundancy notices if applicable |
| | | | July 1 | – All posts filled pending introduction of the new structure |
| | | | | – Begin programme of management development identified by centre |
| | | | Sept 1 | – Launch of new structure |
| Introduce new prices and other changes arising from the business plan; continue existing operation. Undertake budget monitoring with particular emphasis on generating additional income. (Objective 2) Complete full cost analysis. (Objective 3) | Throughout | David Banes Malcolm Browning | April 1 | – Year-end figures completed |
| | | | April 14 | – Phased budget available and implemented |
| | | | May 1 | – All budget-holders notified of actual budgets for the year |
| | | | May 1 | – Priorities for additional income identified and prioritised Monitoring |
| | | | May 1 | – Complete full cost analysis |
| | | | Monthly | – Report to SMG against key budget lines c/o MB |
| | | | Termly | – Finance sub-committee meeting to review financial position Targets |
| | | | | Fees X Other Income X Total Income X |
| | | | | Premises X Maintenance X Food/Med/Educ X |
| | | | | Equip under 1K X |
| Develop Standards of Care Statements and identify standards as a key responsibility of new unit manager posts. (Objective 4) | September | Caroline Nielson | March | – Draft statements agreed |
| | | | May | – Resources identified |
| | | | May | – Training implications of standards identified and introduce September training programme |
| | | | June | – Standards of care identified as key responsibility of new manager posts |
| Release two co-ordinators on a part-time basis to assist in the identification of a new model for curriculum coverage for the 14–19 age group. (Objective 5) | January | Brandon Mills | Sept 1 | – Framework for policy and curriculum map to be confirmed |
| | | | Sept 1 | – Release two co-ordinators for one day a week on termly basis |
| | | | Sept 1 | – Introduce MOVE curriculum to upper unit |
| | | | Sept 1 | – Introduce AAC curriculum model to FE unit |
| | | | Oct 1 | – Review ARR systems c/o VD |
| | | | Jan | – Review PSE provision and revise accordingly |
| | | | April | – Identify new model for curriculum coverage in 14–19 group Implement trial |
| During the period April to June implement the changes already identified as being necessary to achieve FEFC Grade 2. (Objective 6) | June | Vanessa Dutton | April | – Meet with City and Guilds replacement of tutor |
| | | | | – Begin costed maintenance work |
| | | | | – Additional curriculum resources ordered |
| | | | | – Progression aims set at annual reviews |
| | | | May | – Introduction of baseline assessment documentation |
| | | | | – Review links to external accreditation |
| | | | June | – Inspection from FEFC |
| Review existing training programmes and develop these so that they reflect the current needs of individual staff and the business plan. (Objective 7) | May | John McLachlan | Introduce individual training programmes | |
| | | | Develop training programmes – skills of staff with additional extended professional development | |
| | | | Managers | |
| | | | Integrating health practice into scheme | |
| | | | Employ one teacher under the terms of the licensed or graduate scheme | |

The head teacher of Meldreth Manor School was asked to make comments regarding his experience of business planning, which are included below and look back over two years of business planning.

'After two years of being actively involved in the preparation of a business plan for my school I have been able to begin to see that the work involved has many benefits.

Business planning is a process that is deceptive. I feared that I was embarking on a process that was complex and likely to be understood by very few. But, in practice, it has proved to be a simple and effective means of communicating vision to many.

The simplicity, however, conceals the depth of understanding required of all the aspects and influences that create a successful school. The rigours and tools demand of the head teacher a thorough understanding of the features that contribute to success, and hence allow far more wide-ranging and thorough action plans to be designed than is usually possible.

In practical terms I can now examine the business of my school – the achievements of pupils – and plan to make changes on the basis of need, and then consider how budgets are manipulated to provide support.

This can be a liberating experience for a head teacher. I can feel empowered to identify what I wish and need to do, and then cause that change to be financially possible. Other models of planning constrain me to take a predetermined budget and then to allocate it to the best of my abilities.

This liberation and understanding has proven attractive to grant-making trusts. It is recognised that senior managers have planned to ensure the effective use of any monies that are made available to meet a determined need.

Moreover, as an independent school our many purchasers have felt confident in making placements at the school that we have a real understanding of our costs and our future, and can demonstrate skills that ensure our standards are consistently high.'

# Appendix A: Business Plan Format

## INTRODUCTION

The plan should commence with a brief description of the unit, including size, location, type of services, client groups, history, and period covered by the plan.

## ANALYSIS

### 1. Performance Appraisal

**Aim:** To help the reader understand the performance of the unit.

**Include:** Current performance against plan. Tracking of key indicators over time.

### 2. Strengths and Weaknesses

**Aim:** To help the reader understand the unit, in particular its strengths and weaknesses.

**Include:** Strengths and weaknesses audit.

### 3. Environmental Appraisal

**Aim:** To help the reader understand the environment in which the unit operates.

**Include:** SPELT.

### 4. Customers and Services

**Aim:** To help the reader understand the users, purchasers and other service stakeholders and the link with the services offered.

**Include:** Customer segmentation, demand trends, understanding of the purchasing decision. Service financial analysis.

### 5. Competitor/Alternative Provider Analysis

**Aim:** To help the reader appreciate the impact of competitors and further develop understanding of their own school or service.

**Include:** In respect of identified providers, details of services, prices, size, funding, etc.

### 6. Opportunities and Threats

**Aim:** To help the reader understand the opportunities and threats which face the unit.

**Include:** Opportunities and threats arising from the internal and external appraisal, customer and service analysis, etc.

### 7. Summary of Analysis

Concise summary of the current position of the unit together with a view as to the likely future situation assuming no specific management action is taken.

# DIRECTION

## 1. GIVENS

**Aim:** To help the reader appreciate the boundaries within which the plan is prepared.

**Include:** All types of 'givens', whether constraints or restraints.

## 2. AIM STATEMENT

**Aim:** To help the reader understand the purpose of the unit.

**Include:** This statement can be in the form of a traditional mission statement or a statement of purpose, statement of aims or statement of values.

## 3. OBJECTIVES

**Aim:** To provide a clear expression of what the school or service will achieve over the life of the plan.

**Include:** Objectives which are of primary importance.

## 4. STRATEGIES

**Aim:** To help the user understand how the objectives are to be achieved.

**Include:** Details of existing and new strategies which are to be pursued during the period of the plan.

# IMPLEMENTATION

## 1. IMPLEMENTATION PLAN

**Aim:** To ensure that the reader will believe that the plan has been well thought through and is likely to happen.

**Include:** Details of actions required, key dates and responsible staff. Arrangements for monitoring actions and performance during the plan.

## 2. FINANCIAL PLAN

**Aim:** To ensure that the reader understands the financial implications of pursuing the plan.

**Include:** Budgeted profit and loss accounts and cash-flow forecast. As appropriate also include a capital budget and balance sheet.

## 3. CONTINGENCY PLAN

**Aim:** To show that thought has been given to the actions which may be necessary if events do not happen as expected.

**Include:** Details of those factors to which the school or service may be sensitive and the measures available for minimising the impact.

# Appendix B: Revenue Account – Example

| | Budget – Existing Activities | Budget – Additional Strategies | Total | Inflation | Proposed Budget |
|---|---|---|---|---|---|
| **Income** | £ | £ | £ | £ | £ |
| Fees | 1179000 | 55000 | 1234000 | 55500 | 1289500 |
| Sales | 3500 | | 3500 | 300 | 3800 |
| Other Income | 4700 | | 4700 | 300 | 5000 |
| **Total Income** | 1187200 | 55000 | 1242200 | 56100 | 1298300 |
| | | | | | |
| **Expenditure** | | | | | |
| | | | | | |
| Salaries – General | 18460 | | 184600 | 6200 | 190800 |
| Care | 335600 | | 335600 | 11200 | 346800 |
| Teachers | 190300 | 38000 | 228300 | 8100 | 236400 |
| Therapists | 25400 | 4500 | 29900 | 1300 | 31200 |
| Ancillary | 108700 | | 108700 | 4100 | 112800 |
| Employer's N. Insurance | 65200 | 4000 | 69200 | 2800 | 72000 |
| Employer's Pension | 17100 | 1500 | 18600 | 600 | 19200 |
| Agency Staff | 22100 | | 22100 | 700 | 22800 |
| Rates – General | 400 | | 400 | 0 | 400 |
| Rates – Water | 12800 | | 12800 | 400 | 13200 |
| Electricity | 10200 | 300 | 10500 | 400 | 10900 |
| Gas | 10100 | | 10100 | 400 | 10500 |
| Cleaning | 4600 | | 4600 | 200 | 4800 |
| Property Maintenance | 40600 | | 40600 | 1400 | 42000 |
| Food Supplies | 33800 | 2800 | 36600 | 1200 | 37800 |
| Medical Supplies | 2000 | 300 | 2300 | 100 | 2400 |
| Educational Supplies | 8700 | 500 | 9200 | 300 | 9500 |
| Vehicle Running Costs | 15200 | 1000 | 16200 | 600 | 16800 |
| Staff Travel | 1000 | 200 | 1200 | 0 | 1200 |
| Postage | 1100 | 100 | 1200 | 0 | 1200 |
| Stationery & Printing | 3400 | 100 | 3500 | 100 | 3600 |
| Telephone | 5700 | 100 | 5800 | 200 | 6000 |
| Repairs of Equipment | 20900 | | 20900 | 700 | 21600 |
| Advertising | 1600 | | 1600 | 100 | 1700 |
| Sundry | 1200 | | 1200 | 0 | 1200 |
| Depreciation: Property | 13200 | | 13200 | 500 | 13700 |
| Equipment | 6300 | | 6300 | 200 | 6500 |
| Vehicles | 14500 | | 14500 | 500 | 15000 |
| **Total Expenses** | 1156300 | 53400 | 1209700 | 42300 | 1252000 |
| | | | | | |
| **Surplus (Deficit)** | 30900 | 1600 | 32500 | 13800 | 46300 |

# Appendix C: Cash Flow Forecast – Example

| | April | May | June | July | Aug | Sept | Oct | Nov | Dec | Jan | Feb | March | Total |
|---|---|---|---|---|---|---|---|---|---|---|---|---|---|
| Receipts | £ | £ | £ | £ | £ | £ | £ | £ | £ | £ | £ | £ | £ |
| Fees | | | 419400 | | | | | 41900 | | | | 41900 | 1258200 |
| Sales | 300 | 300 | 300 | 300 | 300 | 300 | 300 | 300 | 300 | 300 | 300 | 300 | 3600 |
| Other Income | 400 | 400 | 400 | 400 | 400 | 400 | 400 | 400 | 400 | 400 | 400 | 400 | 4800 |
| **Total Receipts** | **700** | **700** | **420100** | **700** | **700** | **700** | **700** | **420100** | **700** | **700** | **700** | **420100** | **1266600** |
| | | | | | | | | | | | | | |
| **Payments** | | | | | | | | | | | | | |
| Salaries – General | 15900 | 15900 | 15900 | 15900 | 15900 | 15900 | 15900 | 15900 | 15900 | 15900 | 15900 | 15900 | 190800 |
| Care | 28900 | 28900 | 28900 | 28900 | 28900 | 28900 | 28900 | 28900 | 28900 | 28900 | 28900 | 28900 | 346800 |
| Teachers | 19700 | 19700 | 19700 | 19700 | 19700 | 19700 | 19700 | 19700 | 19700 | 19700 | 19700 | 19700 | 236400 |
| Therapists | 2600 | 2600 | 2600 | 2600 | 2600 | 2600 | 2600 | 2600 | 2600 | 2600 | 2600 | 2600 | 31200 |
| Ancillary | 9400 | 9400 | 9400 | 9400 | 9400 | 9400 | 9400 | 9400 | 9400 | 9400 | 9400 | 9400 | 11280 |
| Employer's N. Insurance | 6000 | 6000 | 6000 | 6000 | 6000 | 6000 | 6000 | 6000 | 6000 | 6000 | 6000 | 6000 | 72000 |
| Employer's Pension | 1600 | 1600 | 1600 | 1600 | 1600 | 1600 | 1600 | 1600 | 1600 | 1600 | 1600 | 1600 | 19200 |
| Agency Staff | 1900 | 1900 | 1900 | 1900 | 1900 | 1900 | 1900 | 1900 | 1900 | 1900 | 1900 | 1900 | 22800 |
| Rates – General | 200 | | | | | | 200 | | | | | | 400 |
| Rates – Water | 1100 | 1100 | 1100 | 1100 | 1100 | 1100 | 1100 | 1100 | 1100 | 1100 | 1100 | 1100 | 13200 |
| Electricity | | 2900 | | | 2100 | | | 2600 | | | 3300 | | 10900 |
| Gas | | 100 | | | 2100 | | | 3100 | | | 4200 | | 10500 |
| Cleaning | 400 | 400 | 400 | 400 | 400 | 400 | 400 | 400 | 400 | 400 | 400 | 400 | 4800 |
| Property Maintenance | 3500 | 3500 | 3500 | 3500 | 3500 | 3500 | 3500 | 3500 | 3500 | 3500 | 3500 | 3500 | 42000 |
| Food Supplies | 3600 | 3600 | 3600 | 3600 | 3600 | 3600 | 3600 | 3600 | 3600 | 3600 | 3600 | 3600 | 37800 |
| Medical Supplies | 200 | 200 | 200 | 200 | 200 | 200 | 200 | 200 | 200 | 200 | 200 | 200 | 2400 |
| Educational Supplies | 2500 | 200 | 200 | 200 | 2500 | 200 | 200 | 200 | 2700 | 200 | 200 | 200 | 9500 |
| Vehicle Running Costs | 1400 | 1400 | 1400 | 1400 | 1400 | 1400 | 1400 | 1400 | 1400 | 1400 | 1400 | 1400 | 16800 |
| Staff Travel | 100 | 100 | 100 | 100 | 100 | 100 | 100 | 100 | 100 | 100 | 100 | 100 | 1200 |
| Postage | 100 | 100 | 100 | 100 | 100 | 100 | 100 | 100 | 100 | 100 | 100 | 100 | 1200 |
| Stationery & Printing | 300 | 300 | 300 | 300 | 300 | 300 | 300 | 300 | 300 | 300 | 300 | 300 | 3600 |
| Telephone | 1500 | | | 1500 | | | 1500 | | | 1500 | | | 6000 |
| Repairs of Equipment | 1800 | 1800 | 1800 | 1800 | 1800 | 1800 | 1800 | 1800 | 1800 | 1800 | 1800 | 1800 | 21600 |
| Advertising | 400 | 300 | 100 | 100 | 100 | 100 | 100 | 100 | 100 | 100 | 100 | 100 | 1200 |
| Sundry | 100 | 100 | 100 | 100 | 100 | 100 | 100 | 100 | 100 | 100 | 100 | 100 | 1200 |
| **Total Payments** | 103200 | 103100 | 98900 | 10400 | 101800 | 98900 | 100600 | 104600 | 101400 | 100400 | 106400 | 97100 | 1216800 |
| **Balance B/Forward** | 30000 | −72500 | −174900 | 146300 | 46600 | −54500 | −152700 | −252600 | 62900 | −37800 | −137500 | −243200 | |
| Net Monthly Flow | −102500 | −102400 | 321200 | −99700 | −10110 | −98200 | −99900 | 315500 | −100700 | −99700 | −105700 | 323000 | |
| **Balance C/Forward** | −72500 | −174900 | 146300 | 46600 | −54500 | −152700 | −252600 | 62900 | −37800 | −137500 | −243200 | 79800 | |

# Appendix D: Business Plan Evaluation Summary

**SCOPE – EDUCATION SERVICES**

**BUSINESS PLAN EVALUATION**

**School/College/Service**_____ **Date**_____

The following comments regarding the business plan are intended to complement the evaluation undertaken by governors and line management. The focus is on the quality of the plan and the apparent logic and persuasiveness of the proposed course of action. The wider evaluation aimed at the technical content will be undertaken by those having a detailed knowledge of the sector, service and in many cases the subject of the plan.

| SECTION | CURRENT BUSINESS PLAN EVALUATION | FUTURE PLAN DEVELOPMENT |
|---|---|---|
| **ANALYSIS** | | |
| **Performance** | | |
| **Strengths and Weaknesses** | | |
| **Environment Analysis (SPELT)** | | |
| **Customers and Services** | | |
| **Competitors** | | |
| **Opportunities/Threats** | | |
| **Summary of Analysis** | | |

| SECTION | CURRENT BUSINESS PLAN EVALUATION | FUTURE PLAN DEVELOPMENT |
|---|---|---|
| **DIRECTION**<br><br>**Givens**<br><br>**Aim**<br><br>**Objectives**<br><br>**Strategies** | | |
| **IMPLEMENTATION**<br><br>**Implementation Plan**<br><br>**Financial Plan**<br><br>**Contingency Plan** | | |
| **OVERALL** | | |

# Appendix E: Overhead Transparencies – Masters

BUSINESS PLANNING

Overhead
1.1

**Business planning is...
the process by which resources
and actions are directed at
achieving a strategy selected to
satisfy the objectives and,
ultimately, the mission of an
organisation, department or unit...**

Overhead
1.2

**A business plan is...**
**a document which describes a set**
**of clear actions needed to achieve a**
**desired outcome, set within a**
**summary of the environmental and**
**organisational context in order that**
**the reader may be assured of its**
**realism and integrity...**

Overhead
1.3

**Potential
Benefits
of
Business
Planning**

- LEADS TO IMPROVED PERFORMANCE
- ASSISTS IN DEVELOPING RELATIONSHIPS WITH CUSTOMERS
- PROVIDES A FRAMEWORK FOR DECISION-MAKING
- HELPS REDUCE STRESS THROUGH THE CLARIFICATION OF PRIORITIES
- INTRODUCES LONGER-TERM PERSPECTIVE
- HELPS MANAGERS TO BECOME CREATIVE
- INCREASES COMMITMENT AND OWNERSHIP
- MOTIVATES

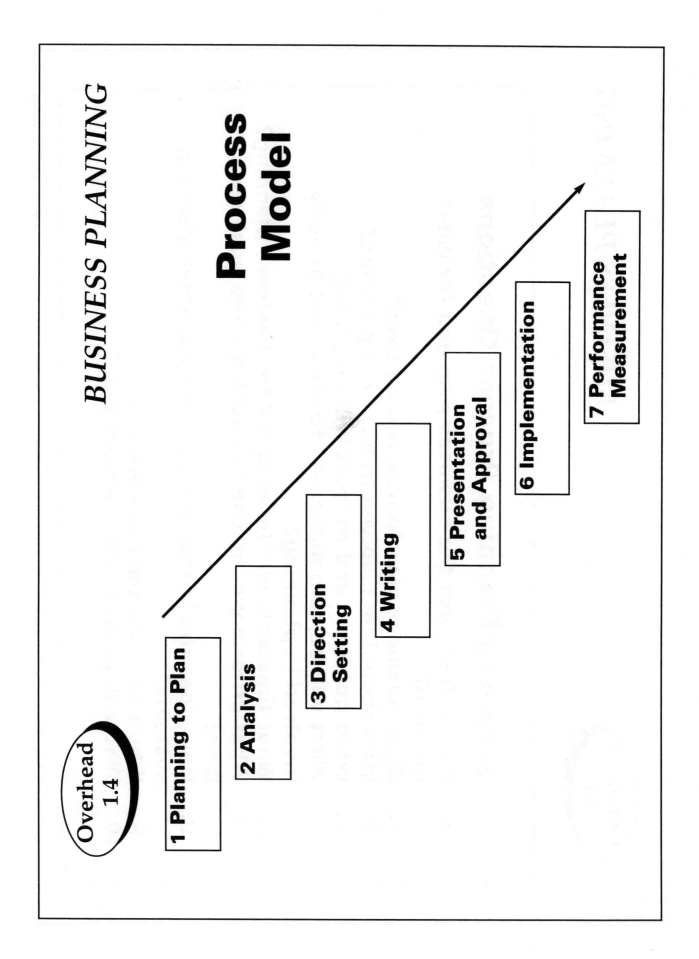

## Business Planning Process Questions

1. Who will receive the business plan and for what purpose?

2. What business plan format will be used?

3. Who should be involved in business planning?

4. What guidance and support will be given?

5. What will be communicated to those not directly involved in planning?

6. What timetable will be adopted for business planning?

7. What criteria will be used to evaluate the business plan?

8. How does the business plan link with other planning systems?

9. Who will write the business plan?

10. Who will present the business plan?

Overhead 3.1

## Analysis – Six Key Questions

1. What do we know about the performance of the school or service?

2. What do we know about how we operate?

3. What do we know about our environment?

4. What do we know about our customers and services?

5. What do we know about competitors or alternative providers?

6. What do we know about opportunities and threats?

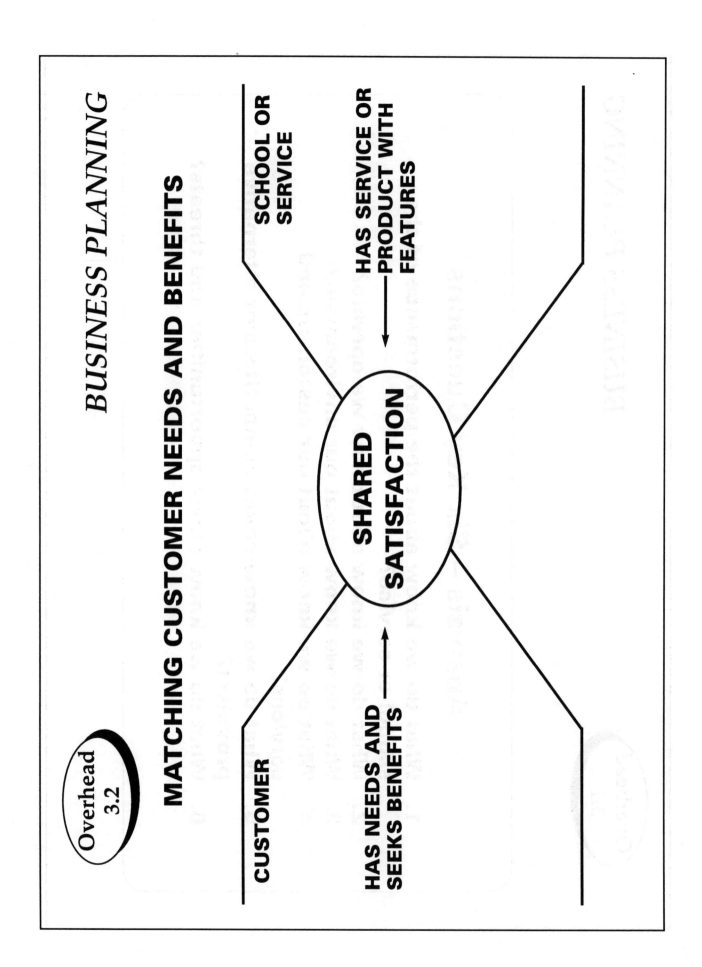

*BUSINESS PLANNING*

Overhead 3.2

**MATCHING CUSTOMER NEEDS AND BENEFITS**

SCHOOL OR SERVICE

HAS SERVICE OR PRODUCT WITH FEATURES

SHARED SATISFACTION

CUSTOMER

HAS NEEDS AND SEEKS BENEFITS

*BUSINESS PLANNING*

What stakeholder groups should be included in the analysis?

For each stakeholder group →

1. How might this group be meaningfully segmented?

2. What needs do stakeholders within this group have?

3. What features of the service do they value?

4. To what extent do the identified needs appear to be met?

5. What involvement do stakeholders within this group have in the decision to select the school or service?

6. What initially attracts stakeholders to this school or service?

7. How satisfied is this stakeholder group?

81

Overhead 3.4

# Competitor or Alternative Provider Questions

1. What services do they offer?

2. Who funds or purchases from them?

3. Where is their market-place?

4. Why do their customers use them?

5. What do we know about them (size, premises, staff base, strengths and weaknesses, performance, reputation, how they operate, prices, etc.)?

6. What appears to be their approach to competition?

7. Is anything known about their future intentions?

# BUSINESS PLANNING

**EVALUATION MATRIX**

| Decision Factors | 1. | 2. | Strategy Options 3. | 4. |
|---|---|---|---|---|
|  |  |  |  |  |
|  |  |  |  |  |
|  |  |  |  |  |
|  |  |  |  |  |

Overhead 5.1

# *BUSINESS PLANNING*

| Strategy | Actions | Key Dates | Responsible Person | Monitoring Arrangements |
|---|---|---|---|---|
| Introduce staff development programme by 31/12/98 | Needs analysis | 31/1/98 | Deputy | Management team agenda |
| | Consultation | 31/5/98 | Head teacher | Item on staff evaluation |
| | Design | 31/7/98 | | |
| | Pilot | 30/9/98 | | |

**IMPLEMENTATION SUMMARY**

# Bibliography

Barnard, H. and Walker, P. (1994) *Strategies for Success (A Self-Help Guide for Strategic Planning for Voluntary Organisations)*. London: NCVO Publications.

DES (1988) *Local Management of Schools*. London: HMSO.

DES (1991) *Local Management of Schools: Further Guidance. Circular 7/9.* London: HMSO.

DfEE (1996) *Setting Targets to Raise Standards (1996) – A Survey of Good Practice*. London: HMSO.

DoE Local Management of Schools: The Future Framework. Consultation Document DFE

DFEE (1995) *Benchmarking School Budgets (1995): Sharing Good Practice*. London: NCVO Publications.

Knight, B. (1993) *Financial Management for Schools (The Thinking Manager's Guide)*. Oxford: Heineman.

LGMB (1991) *A Business Plan for the Nineties (The Application of Business Planning)*. London: LGMB.

Martin, N. and Smith, C. (1993) *Planning for the Future (An Introduction to Business Planning for Voluntary Organisations)*. London: NCVO Publications

Puffitt, R. (1993) *Business Planning and Marketing (A Guide for the Local Government Cost Centre Manager)*. Harlow: Longmans.

Puffit, R., Stolen, B. and Winkley, D. (1992) *Business Planning for Schools*. Harlow: Longmans.

Richardson, B. and Richardson, R. (1992) *Business Planning (An Approach to Strategic Management)*. London: Pitman.